THE PAINTER LADY
Grace Carpenter Hudson

Grace Carpenter Hudson
1865 — 1937

THE
PAINTER
LADY
Grace
Carpenter
Hudson

SEARLES R. BOYNTON D.D.S.

ii Interface California Corporation

EUREKA

TO MARGE

The other lady in my life, and to our three blessings
Paige, Kevin, and Tambi

CONTENTS

Preface   iv

Acknowledgements   xi

Prologue   3

CHAPTER   I   THE EARLY YEARS
Art Education and a First Marriage   13

CHAPTER   II   THE BUDDING CAREER
An Enduring Second Marriage and a First Major Work   23

CHAPTER   III   MAJOR ACHIEVEMENTS
Little Mendocino and the World's Fair   27

CHAPTER   IV   THE CENTURY'S END
Growth and Recognition in the World of Art   39

CHAPTER   V   TRAVELS AND A NEW CENTURY
Travels to Hawaii, Chicago, and Europe   53

CHAPTER   VI   BACK TO CALIFORNIA
New Canvases of the Pomo   65

CHAPTER   VII   THE LATER YEARS
Life in the Sun House   73

CHAPTER   VIII   THE FINAL YEARS
Completion of a Life Work   87

Plates   91

Catalog Raisonné   157

Index   185

PREFACE

READING *The Painter Lady* will be an adventure into the life and era of Grace Carpenter Hudson, as well as her loves. Her loves comprised not only unity and affection for her husband, but her uncommon devotion to the Pomo Indians of northern California. The reader will share in Grace Hudson's joy and enthusiam as she captured their beauty, customs, dress, mores, religions, lifestyle, and heartwarming shyness. In addition, one will learn from the heritage of the Indians and Grace Hudson much about the pioneer life and history of Mendocino County, California and the surrounding region.

The Painter Lady offers the reader a trip backwards in time to a period of simpler life. As one glances through the book for the first time, they will be pleasantly enthused by the wealth of paintings accomplished in almost 45 years of constant dedication. At each succeeding reading, however, the depth and beauty will grow, and the reader will find himself or herself coming to know not only the Pomo Indians, but the artist.

In our family, we did, indeed, come to know the Painter Lady very well. With all the tremendous research done, there still remain many unanswered questions about Grace. Many of these deal with her personal life, a life as private and intimate as were most at the end of the last century.

We know that Grace Hudson's husband, John, rode into town from Tennessee to become the most sought-after bachelor in Ukiah, and that Grace and he were married a few months later. We know that the union produced no children, but can only speculate that this was by choice or that children were not possible. We may presume without certainty that Grace and John experienced marital difficulties after 1900, and that this resulted in her extended separation through travel, but her reasons for leaving for Hawaii were not clear. Neither was John Hudson's faltering interest in medicine easily explainable.

These, and many more gaps, remain in understanding completely the life of Grace Carpenter Hudson.

This biography was researched with an almost outrageous enthusiasm and zeal. The book has been completed with the insistant belief that almost any reader would be intrigued and delighted by the story of an artist with the talent of Grace Hudson. To each person, young or old, there awaits the reward of discovery. There is something for everyone — historian, children and adults in search of folklore, fans of the Native Americans with whom Grace's life was so intricately woven, and especially those who would seek to appreciate her art.

Just how great Grace Carpenter Hudson's talent was remains to the reader to assess. Time will evaluate her work and worth, as it must every person's contribution to society. Wherever she is placed, she has undeniably given each of us a priceless legacy to enjoy.

ACKNOWLEDGEMENTS

ART IS SOMETHING that has been treasured throughout history, and I became very aware that not only is the art itself treasured, but also much of the interest surrounding it. In the beginning, many difficulties confronted me. As the months passed and the research mounted, there were many people that shared both their knowledge and their treasures with me. For these many, many friends, I am indeed grateful.

First and foremost among these was Melissa Carpenter Kendrick — my librarian, my historian, my research assistant, my inspiration, my reassurance, and my friend — without whose help this book would never have been a reality. In six wonderful years of afternoon chats and evening telephone conversations, there was never a parting without Melissa's words of encouragement or expressions of enthusiasm. Whenever I felt I had captured the entire story of Grace Hudson, Melissa's bag of tricks always produced another anecdote or some interesting family keepsake. Each gem came forth from a keen mind and a flawless memory.

It was with great sadness that I learned of Melissa's passing in October of 1975. She was laid to rest in the Hudson family plot. During the few weeks which remained of her life, Melissa completed the necessary arrangements for the Hudson estate to become the property of the City of Ukiah. Generations to come will be grateful forever for the City of Ukiah's, and Melissa's, foresight. Her joy in reading the manuscript and knowing the book would someday be published has now been realized.

To the many art galleries of the San Francisco bay area, I am indebted, especially those on Sutter Street. For the late Fred Maxwell's advice, "Take your time and do it thoroughly, she's the greatest artist that ever lived in California;" for Howard Willoughby's insight and frequent words of assurance; for the greeting of "Dr. Hudson" from Joan Wortsman and Wilma Steward which never failed to brighten my day; and for Mary Hunter's optimistic inquiries, "When is the book going to be finished?"; to all these people I am grateful.

Research information was made available to me through many sources, but notably the Newberry Library in Chicago, the California State Library in Sacramento, the Oakland Museum, the Bancroft Library, the Library of Congress, the San Francisco Public Library, the Mechanic's Institute Library, the California Historical Society Library, the Mendocino County Library, and the Ukiah Daily Journal's archives.

Many of the photographs of paintings and family portraits were reproduced from glass emulsion slides and old negatives taken by A. O. Carpenter, the artist's father. For a winter of untiring patience against some extremely difficult conditions, I wish to thank Chris Towne, without whose help some priceless photographs may have been lost to antiquity. To the many artists of the camera that made the color plates of this book possible, I also give my thanks.

Lewis Frabrache, Dr. Joseph Baird, Jr., Dr. James Holliday, Mrs. Frederick Whitridge, Mrs. David Potter, Mrs. Marjorie Arkelian, Miss Sharon

Cantrell, Mrs. Frank Prentice, Mr. Al Thrasher, Mr. and Mrs. Roy Farrington Jones, and Mrs. Beth Bittner are only a few of the many people that helped me with research or opened a door to additional information that helped make the book an accurate account of the artist's life.

For the many hours, days, weeks, and months that I have stolen from my family I hope this book will repay the debt. Each of them — Paige, Kevin, and Tambi, but mostly Marge — have, on more than one occasion, had Grace Hudson's life for breakfast, lunch, and dinner. I appreciate their indulgence.

There are many people too numerous to mention that have shared their art collections for this book, taken special effort to aid me in my research, and opened their doors to my questions. I hope that each and every one will feel that they have had a share in the applause.

THE PAINTER LADY
Grace Carpenter Hudson

PROLOGUE

Ho! for California. At last we are on our way. We are only seven miles from home and with a little good luck we may someday reach the "promised land." The trip has been talked of for so long and the preparation has gone on under so many adverse conditions that to be ready to start is something of an event.

A. O. Carpenter, Helen Carpenter,
May Carpenter

SO BEGINS, on May 26, 1857, the diary of Grace Carpenter Hudson's mother, Helen McCowen Carpenter. From its start in the Territory of Kansas, then an armed camp in the struggle between pro-slavery and anti-slavery settlers, this remarkable account of the McCowen and Carpenter families' trek to California covers more than 90 pages. A young, newly-wedded bride, Helen kept her diary while on the trail in hope that it might enable later travelers to the West to find a safer course, shallower crossings, an uncontaminated watering hole, better grazing for teams and stock, or more plentiful game supplies. As years passed, it served instead to supply numerous unusual experiences for sharing with her four children. Copies of the diary, which form an invaluable record of the western migration in the 1850's, have been placed in the California State Library, Huntington Library, and the Newberry Library.

The McCowen-Carpenter party arrived in Grass Valley in Placer County, California on October 7, 1857 after a trip of some five months' duration. There the party separated, with the Carpenters remaining in Grass Valley while the McCowens journeyed onward to Potter Valley in Mendocino County, California. After traveling so far together, it might seem strange that Thomas and Amily McCowen would continue their journey without their daughter and son-in-law; Helen was in no condition to continue the journey.

The honeymoon trip across the plains had indeed been difficult, but evidently was not without time for a few of the things that occupy the minds of young lovers. While her husband, Aurelius O. "Reel" Carpenter, was working in the mining fields of Selby Flat, Helen was preparing for the arrival of their first-born child. On March 15, 1858, a daughter named May was born. Looking back over the previous nine months it becomes easy to understand why the mountain road, the rocks, the dust, the river crossings and the many countless inconveniences of the trail were so emphasized in Helen's diary.

By the spring of 1858, California's mining camps were full of men seeking their fortunes. Reel, being from the Midwest, probably felt there was a better future on top of the ground than underneath. He invested his earnings in a small place known as the Hill's Ranch, near Grass Valley. The ensuing months were spent ranching, teaming, as well as typesetting in the *Telegraph* newspaper office.

The newspaper business was not a new trade to Carpenter. Until the time he was 14 years of age, Reel attended school six months of the year. He then entered the office of *The Windman County Democrat* which was owned by his step-father, George W. Nichols. It was during those years that he mastered the newspaper business and prepared the foundation for much of the rest of his life. When he was 19,

3

he was briefly a member of the surveying party that helped lay out Topeka, the future capital of Kansas. When a printing office was established in Lawrence, he had the distinction of setting the first stick of type for the earliest newspaper in the territory, *The Herald of Freedom*, and later helped found still another publication, *The Free State*.

The Carpenters quickly became part of life in Grass Valley. Early in 1859, Reel was appointed road overseer for the region. He was the type of man, however, who found it difficult to stay in one place or to do the same thing for any period of time. By November, his daughter May was 19 months old and able to travel, and the little family decided it was time for her to become acquainted with her grandparents in Potter Valley. Reel resigned his office, sold the ranch and prepared for the journey to Mendocino County, where they would live with relatives and friends.

The 200-mile trek was undertaken with another family, which consisted of a father, mother, and their four children. They were outfitted with a heavy freight wagon full of household goods and an ordinary farm wagon. Both vehicles were drawn by oxen, with seven yoke in all.

Farming implements and the winter's supply of food were purchased in Sacramento. While still in the city, the first discomfort of the journey appeared in the form of a rainstorm. Their family wagon was covered, but the other was without any protection from the elements. The group decided that ten dollars could not be spared for a wagon ducking sheet, but when a last minute trip was made for some forgotten article, a ten dollar gold piece was found on the sidewalk.

Suitably protected from the bad weather, they began the next leg of their journey. A ride through the busiest street in the state capitol in an ox wagon, followed by a huge, white-sheeted baggage wagon, created such interest in passersby that the group felt like a "wild west show." It took many years for the women of the party to see the comedy in the episode, but it was later referred to as "our triumphal march through Sacramento."

The adobe land west of Sacramento became sticky from the steady rainfall, and it was not long before the wagon wheels were solid masses of clay. For a distance, double-teaming was necessary. By nine o'clock that evening, five miles had been covered. Drenched with rain, bedraggled and covered to the knees with mud, they reached the Tule House, their intended night's stopping point, but were refused a place to stay by the innkeeper. After a miserable evening spent huddled in a shed by a forbidden fire, the group continued its journey westward in the grey and misty light of dawn.

Eventually they reached Putah Creek canyon in the foothills of the Coast Range Mountains. With more than 100 miles to go and with no road except as made by nature, they decided to leave the big wagons and continue with only those things that seemed necessary in the smaller ones. Days continued gloomy and wet. Many places were so rough and steep that it was necessary for everyone to walk. Obtaining hay for the oxen grew serious. The winter supply of flour, as well as the moss and small twigs of young trees were cut down for the cattle to browse on. Near Berriesse Valley, six head of cattle gave out and were left with a man to feed and care for them during the winter.

Not all the residents at trailside were as inhospitable as the innkeeper at Tule House. An evening stop at the Buck Horn ranch helped restore the party's faith in their fellow man. The owner moved his bedding to the hay stack and the travelers took possession of his cabin for the night. Although the cabin door had no hinges and had never been hung, and the women were somewhat fearful of a bear that the rancher claimed had been molesting his stock, they were too fatigued to remain awake and soon fell asleep on the hard puncheon floor. The next morning they

learned that the bear had come near enough to the cabin to scent the owner on the hay stack. As the traveling party departed, they followed his tracks in the soft earth of the road. They measured 13 inches in length.

Upon reaching Big Valley, the road improved and would near the shore of Clear Lake. Vast flocks of wild geese and ducks circled in every direction but kept out of gun shot distance.

The last few miles of the incredible journey posed a final obstacle for the tired little band. Just ten miles from Potter Valley, the sketchy road dwindled to merely a steep trail. Once again, belongings were gone over and the most necessary ones sorted out. Before two miles had been traveled, things had to be removed from the wagon and carried up bit by bit, for the cattle were exerting their full strength in pulling the empty wagon. Night was approaching and it was snowing. Suddenly, to the relief of everyone in the group, a familiar trio of figures came into view through the storm. Helen Carpenter's uncle, Sam Mewhinney, and two of his boys appeared leading three saddle horses. Later they learned that an itinerant minister bound for Potter Valley, whom the party had met a few days previously, had carried the news of their arrival.

Leaving all of their belongings piled in the wagon with a gun's muzzle pointed outward to give would-be thieves the idea of a trap, the trip was continued with the women on horseback riding sidesaddle in men's saddles and carrying their children on their laps. Men walked along the sides of precipitous gulches and down steep hills. They frequently looked up at the fearful women, saying "Hold tight and you'll get there." In all the long journey across the plains, nothing had happened to compare with this.

· · · · ·

The Carpenters, who had left almost all their worldly possessions strewn along the trail, quickly discovered that many privations and every conceivable inconvenience awaited them in their new homeland. Although Indian women and men brought their things from the top of the mountain several weeks later, their stove was left with the first wagon and all cooking had to be done in Dutch ovens or frying pans. Many months passed before there was another stove. Farming implements were scarce. Seed was scarce. Teams were scarce. Indeed, a scarcity of everything that seemed necessary to human enjoyment marked their first days in Potter Valley, except hospitality and friendliness. Grain served as the basic food element, and their diet was composed largely of boiled wheat and milk. One woman in the valley remarked that she ate wheat, drank wheat, and smoked wheat. It kept them in such a good state of health, however, that the settlement of a physician was discouraged for many years.

Houses generally were built of logs and had one room with a puncheon, or split timber, floor. Doors were constructed of clapboards with huge wooden hinges and long wooden latches lifted by a buckskin thong. If a shelf was desired, holes were bored in the logs of the wall and large pegs driven into them to support the shelf. Bedsteads were built in a corner of the house against the wall, with only a post, or horse bedstead, standing free. A table of clapboards and some three-legged stools completed the furnishings of a typical pioneer home.

There was always a great deal of borrowing back and forth, and Helen Carpenter only remembered one instance of a refusal to lend when a friend wanted to borrow. A child sent to borrow candle molds was told, "We don't lend our candle molds, but, if you bring your tallow over, we'll help you run your candles." A few days later the candle mold owner wished to borrow an augur for the framing of a barn. He was told, "We don't lend our augur, but, if you will bring your

Carpenter residence in Potter Valley, 1859 Birthplace of Grace Hudson

5

barn over, we'll help you frame it."

Horses provided the only mode of travel, and there were fearless riders even among the ladies. A few were quite at home on a horse without saddle or bridle. With merely a rope looped around the horse's nose, they rode at breakneck speed, ran races, and jumped ditches and creeks without a thought of danger or accident.

When the petite blonde sister of Mr. Potter, after whom the region derived its name, wanted a horse, she did not hesitate to throw a lasso on a bronco, blind and saddle him, then, with a hackamore instead of bridle, she would mount, remove the blind, and stand prepared for whatever might happen. If the horse proved to be wild, the boys said, "Miss Paddy will stay with him." That she accomplished such a feat riding sidesaddle in a men's saddle was a wonder to all beholders.

On one occasion, the same young lady rode from Potter Valley to Healdsburg, a distance of some 70 miles in one day. She attended a ball the same evening.

Wild animals were abundant in Potter Valley, often causing loss of sleep as well as property. When a cabin was built, the mice moved in at once and availed themselves of both food and clothing. Crickets set to work on clothing and book bindings (if there were any books available). Hawks, mink, skunk, and raccoon looked after the poultry, coyotes watched the sheep; panthers, or puma, did not ignore the calves and young colts, while grizzly bear were content to feed on hogs unless lamb was available, since mutton was much preferred to pork.

The skunks showed less fear of man than any other of the animals. During the day they were seen walking abroad, their plume-like tails undulating in graceful curves, now aloft, now sweeping the ground. Soon after lamps were out at night, the little patter of their feet could be heard crossing the floor and climbing into cupboards and shelves to sample any edibles within reach.

Bears often marauded, returning two or three times in a single evening, taking a hog each time. Hunts were occasionally successful and resulted in several hundred pounds of meat. Reel Carpenter was told that the paws were among the choicest bits of the bear. There was some remonstrance in the kitchen, but after several hours effort to prepare it, one was cooked. When placed on the table, Helen had taken great care that it was placed right side up on the platter. A single look was enough even for Reel.

Life in the valley was not without its light moments. As Christmas drew near in 1859, two bachelors not known for their especially-tidy household—poultry, hogs, and cattle frequented their cabin—sent verbal invitations for a grand ball to be given at their residence, the adobe. The settlers had been so busy preparing for the winter that there had been no time for making acquaintances, nor for any sociability. For this reason, the ball was looked forward to as a great event.

As the day approached, the mountains had a cap of snow. George McCowen, John and Hugh Mewhinney, and Reel and Helen Carpenter departed for the ball at a brisk gallop. Since all were excellent riders, they fairly flew, splashing through puddles of water left by the recent storm, jumping gullies, fording streams and crossing fields. Before nightfall, they arrived at the door of the adobe, a low, substantial structure with half of the valley for a front yard. The animals were tied to the corral fence and the party went inside.

A pile of dingy blankets heaped in one corner plainly showed the effort to which the bachelors had gone to remove the beds from the "ballroom." A circular, tin-backed pocket looking glass hung on the wall near a red cow's tail. In it was hanging a coarse comb minus most of its teeth. An open fireplace threw out a genial warmth that was acceptable to the benumbed fingers of the riders. The acting hostess remarked, "I'm awful glad you come. There wouldn't have been enough for a cotillion if you hadn't."

A hasty glance took in the ballroom appointments. On either side of the doors were candles held in place on the wall by stout nails. Two candles on the mantel stood in holders made of big, yellow biscuits with a bitumen crust that, as candle holders, were quite satisfactory. If viewed, however, as an article of diet, they cast an unfavorable impression on the bachelors' culinary achievements.

Moses Briggs with his fiddle and Bart with a banjo sat perched in chairs on a table in the corner of the room. As the banjo plunked the couples swung and turned, firelight on the passing faces weaving fantastic, ever-changing shadows on the group. The Schotische, round dances, and reel continued to the small hours of the morning. Supper followed and those standing about the temporary table did justice to the bachelors' fare. It was rumored by those present that there had been some outside assistance in the kitchen.

Because the hour was late, and everyone was now feeling well acquainted, no one wished to break their neck on a homeward ride in the dark. They gathered about the fire and talked about experiences with bucking horses and grizzly bears until daylight. In a sudden lull in the conversation, the munching of the hay in the manger in the next room gave welcome to the spirit of Christmas in Potter Valley.

By now, the candles on the wall had died away, and those on the mantel showed a beautiful tracery of tallow over the biscuits. In the subdued light of the fire the revelers' spell was broken by the entrance of someone who announced that it was "gettin' daylight and time to go home."

. . . . .

The winter of 1859-1860 brought a great deal of suffering and many deaths to the Pomo Indians of Potter Valley. Great herds of Spanish horses and cattle were everywhere and had destroyed almost the entire oat crop before the grain had matured. Bands of the settlers' pigs turned the earth in search of edible roots, but also fed abundantly on the clover, acorns, and manzanita berries which comprised the staff of life for the Indians. There was little left for them to eat except the larvae of the yellowjackets, the summer caterpillars, and the buckeyes. With the bow and arrow, they occasionally obtained a bird, a squirrel, or, if lucky, a rabbit, for the white men's guns made it difficult to catch any large game. When stock died, no matter what the cause, the Indians eagerly carried off the carcasses for food. On occasions, to keep from starving, they drove off cattle and horses from the settlers' stock. Whenever this occurred, an angry party of settlers would gather to pursue the desperate, pitiful thieves.

The Indians were willing to work, even when pay was nothing more than a good meal. Because they were unfamiliar with white men's ways, their labor was frequently carried out so slowly and clumsily that it often resulted in broken shovel handles or marred and broken axes, and the white settlers were inclined to feel that the Indians had the best of the bargain.

Some of the Pomos learned to help with household chores, such as washing. Aside from the time it took to do the work, the number of persons that they brought along to be fed, the constant supervision—they frequently had to be told when to quit rubbing and when to wring out—the work was generally satisfactory but quite a strain on a housewife's patience.

The Indians were superstitious on many matters. They had a great fear of darkness, for example. All work had to stop early in the day to allow them enough time to reach home before sundown. If they were somewhat late, they traveled home on the run.

Many of the pioneers were not in a position to help themselves, let alone the Indians. Even the most generous had little to divide. Any food obtained from outside the valley had to be packed 75 miles on mules.

Some settler families of the area sacrificed to help care for the Indians, however, and a few Pomos became lifelong friends of their benefactors. No better example can be given than the actions of the Mewhinney family, especially Sarah Mewhinney, who was benevolent to a fault. Indians never left her house hungry; often they left with food to carry to the old or disabled at home. The sick not only had her sympathy, she often went to the *rancheria*, or village, to nurse them. Fortunately, the Mewhinney family was well able to allow full scope to "Aunt" Sarah's generosity and good will.

Writing in the February, 1893 issue of the *Overland Monthly*, Helen Carpenter described some of her first experiences from the period of her life when she lived with the native Californians of Potter Valley:

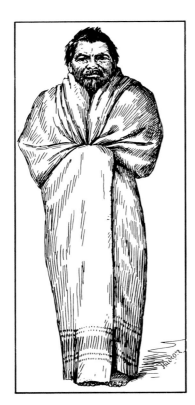

My first caller after entering the valley was Captain John, chief of the Be-lo-kia. *He was a finely musculared Indian, broad of shoulder and nearing the meridian of life. He was clad in his very best, and I must confess I was not much impressed with his greatness from a dress standpoint. A large gray blanket did duty for a full suit and was kept neatly in place without hook, pin, or string.*

. . . Shoes he has never worn. If you ask the reason he will put his immense foot on exhibition, saying la mismo oso *(like a bear's!). In after years he discarded the blanket and made use of any cast-off garments that were procurable, hats meeting with less favor than any other article of dress. A sombrero several sizes too small for his immense head and shaggy locks did make John look a trifle more civilized, but failed to improve his general appearance. John is a born comedian and humorist. His friends get the benefit of all the humorous incidents of the valley. He makes a very enjoyable pantomime of his encounter with a grizzly bear which almost cost him his life. He is never apathetic, never morose, as were most of his people. He was never too tired or with business affairs to joke and make merry at his own expense or that of his friends.*

In the early settlement of the valley, the Captain attached himself to a pioneer family in a very quiet but persistent manner. He adopted the family name and for years has been known as "Indian John Mewhinney." Day after day and month after month found him at his post (the gate post). A good dinner fully compensated him for a walk of four miles and hours of waiting, but John was sure of much more if he performed the slightest duty. The good lady of the house never permitted him to go away empty-handed and he allowed no account to run "one day after date."

. . . Once a wave of unhappiness swept into the Captain's casa causing Anita, the mother of his family many heartaches; however, John, not unlike many of his white brethren under similar circumstances lost neither his temper nor his jocularity. One cold, disagreeable morning Anita took her basket and muchacho, and sallied forth to gather acorns to increase their supply of pinole for the winter.

Several miles were traveled before the basket was filled and the poor little baby grew very tired of being laced so tightly in his basket and dangling on his mother's back being blinded by the wind and bright sunshine. When she reached the rancheria she was very much tired but quickened her steps as she saw the smoke rising from her casa. She thought only of the one who had kindled the fire for her comfort, her own jolly John.

Upon entering the casa, she found John sitting cosily by the fire with a bride at his side. The beads that he had given to the choice of his youth, the simple giving of which made them husband and wife, had during her absence been given to another. Anita was a divorced woman. John's only charge against her was, 'Too mucho Viejo!' Poor old Anita's wrinkled face pleaded guilty to the charge.

Anita looked at the two, then unstrapping John's baby and taking it from the basket, laid its naked body on the ground and set her heel upon its neck. Life was soon gone from the small body. Anita departed with a look of undying hatred and took up residence with the family of her son-in-law, Santa Ana. In after years she was much devoted to her little grandson, Samwy, and seemed a very affectionate grandmother, but she never forgave Captain John.

. . . In later years Captain John came at longer intervals. His back is much bowed with age, his step has lost its elasticity, and his almost sightless eyes make it difficult for him to leave home unattended. . . . If a Pomo Indian is capable of gratitude (which I doubt) probably John is grateful for past favors, although no intimation of the fact has ever escaped him. But he is so much superior to his fellows in many ways that he is a general favorite regardless of his faults. For many years I have tried to teach him to say thank you but his accomplishments in that line are a total failure. The nearest approach to it is 'This dinner good.' . . .

John would often stand peering over the gate gently coughing. 'Come in, you old beggar. Are we not friends?' Will your Indian instincts never permit you to speak instead of coughing to make me aware of your presence? After our long acquaintance will you never enter my gate without an invitation? We are friends; come in. The lesson you have taught me in cheerfulness is worth more than all the bread you will ever eat.

. . . . .

The years between the Carpenters' arrival in Potter Valley and the birth of their twin daughter Grace and son Grant proved to hold the fullest meaning of the word "settlers" for the struggling family. They were indeed the pilgrims of Mendocino County in northwestern California.

Winter of 1859 had come and gone, and spring of 1860 brought the first invitation to everyone in the valley to gather for a working bee, an event much like a barn raising: part toil, part festival. Preparation for the great occasion required food to be cooked for several days in advance. Pies, cakes, cookies, and bread were baked and a large number of chickens and a couple of young pigs were sent to block by way of assuring that no one would depart from the day's activities in hungry disappointment.

On the morning of the event, furniture was removed from the house to make room for the quilters, food preparation, and the dancing to follow. People began arriving at an early hour; it seemed that no one stayed at home.

While the ladies busied themselves "putting in a quilt," the men cleared brush, cut wood, and split rails. Talent for such work began to emerge and it required considerable finesse to allocate the proper jobs to the available skills.

As the hour for dinner approached, a large table was prepared under the shade of some tall oak trees. The men were fed first, giving the women more time for socializing and gossip before returning to their quilting and, later, the preparing of food for supper.

By the time the evening meal was ready for the table, the "worm fence" of split rails was finished, several loads of wood had been hauled in, and the brush was piled and ready for burning. The quilting had been completed as well, with several women stitching the edges after it had been removed from the frame.

After supper, the older folks and the children headed for home while the younger set stayed for dancing. Mr. Leonard played the fiddle, and by three o'clock in the morning everything edible had been disposed of by those who remained.

The largest activity in the valley each year was the Fourth of July celebration, and any mention of life and social events among the early settlers of the area would not be complete if a description was not included.

The first of these annual events took place in 1860. By June, a small group gathered at the home of Helen and Reel Carpenter to make plans for the coming activities. Although everyone agreed that some kind of patriotic demonstration was desirous, they were somewhat undecided as to the nature of their effort. An attempt to practice some songs resulted in total failure, for the settlers knew more about hard work than they did about musical harmony. In a short time, however, a loosely-structured program was agreed upon, and a general notice was sent to all residents of the valley.

Two valley residents, Mr. Van Nader and Mr. McCowen, being quite clever, chopped down a tree, sawed from it a round section, and proceeded to hollow the wooden block out. McCowen provided a buckskin head for the round and strung it tight with rawhide strings of buckskin. They were rewarded for their efforts with a bass drum of sorts.

The group met in a popular spot, Neil's Grove. When all was ready, a procession formed that was led toward the grove by the drum, in the hands of Mr. Van Nader, and the fiddle, played by Mr. Leonard. A more colorful gathering could not have taken place in any other frontier town across the nation.

At the grove, Helen Carpenter and Mrs. Fuller sang *America* with patriotic fervor. Thad Dashiell read the Declaration of Independence, and Reel Carpenter favored the crowd with his key-note address. The program ended to the strained sound of the *Star Spangled Banner*, sung by the two impromptu singers with both attempting the melody. Some considered later that the melody might have been helped if they had included a drum accompaniment by Mr. Van Nader.

Like any such occasion, the highlight of the gathering was its food. Picnic baskets had been filled to overflowing. Suppertime was filled with a mixture of conversation, running children, and a general sharing of warmth among those who attended. A platform had been prepared nearby, and everyone danced to the music of Mose Briggs and Helen Carpenter, some until they were too tired to continue.

. . . . .

During the Civil War years, the valley was divided politically along the lines drawn by the warring North and South. Residents of the upper valley favored the Southern secessionists while those in the lower valley, including the Carpenters and Mewhinneys, leaned politically towards the Union. Feelings became so intense that separate schools were established at each end of Potter Valley, insuring that "improper" beliefs did not contaminate the minds of each respective group's young people. Cool heads prevailed, however, and the only formal violence between the factions was an occasional argument.

After the assassination of President Lincoln, the situation worsened and Potter Valley became a seething political cauldron. If the residents had been in one of the seceded states, their views could not have been more forceful. Although the valley was superficially peaceful, some felt that any overt act might cause bloodshed. A small company of United States soldiers from the San Francisco Presidio were dispatched to the valley and made three arrests. Miss Hattie Buster, a teacher in the upper district, was arrested for spitting on the American flag and trampling it underfoot. Thad Dashiell and Jack McCall were arrested for rejoicing in the death of the President.

Miss Buster was reprimanded and discharged, but Dashiell and McCall were taken to Alcatraz and packed sand there for several months before being released. Some years later, Dashiell was scorned by one of his political party for scratching his ticket, to which he was heard to reply indignantly, "I packed sand for the privilege of expressing *my* opinion."

School teachers' employment prospects changed as the political winds blew back and forth between the Black Republicans and the Secessionists, but Helen McCowen Carpenter had become well established as the school "marm" of Potter Valley. By 1865, four years had passed since the first school began in the area. At first, classes had been held on the ground floor of Henry Randlett's cabin, then a formal schoolhouse was constructed. Because travel on foot or horseback was difficult during the winter months, classes were only offered during the spring and summer. During the fall every available hand was needed at home for the harvest.

Regretfully, Helen made the school board aware of her pending absence from the classroom for the spring term. Her condition made it apparent that she would be busy at home with the birth and rearing of her second child throughout the spring and summer. On February 21, 1865, the *Ukiah Herald* announced the arrival of not one, but *two* young Carpenters:

We are informed that our friend and former fellow townsman, A. O. Carpenter, Esq., has recently been favored by the acquisition of two typos in one installment. There can scarcely be any disagreement in the household, as the mother has, in this instance, favored her liege lord with one of each sex—a bouncing boy and a bright, rosy-cheeked girl. So far as we are concerned, whilst we should feel awful proud, we would nevertheless prefer that such presents should come in broken doses. Mother and children are doing as well as could be expected under the circumstances. Haven't heard from Carpenter as yet!

The boy was named Grant and the girl, Grace.

The eight years following Helen and Reel Carpenter's marriage had been ones of struggle, inconvenience, and hardship. There were times that the mere necessities of food and shelter were not easily obtainable. However, there were always a few things for which they could be thankful; they had been surrounded by friends as warm as any young couple could wish. They had become parents of three healthy children and owned land that produced more food than their family could consume. Potter Valley, which had been a raw wilderness when the Mewhinneys and Carpenters had arrived, was rapidly becoming settled. Newcomers were obliged to purchase, rather than homestead, new land, and the future contained bright promise for everyone, especially the Carpenter family.

CHAPTER I

THE EARLY YEARS

Art Education and a First Marriage

GRACE AND GRANT'S acquaintance with the Pomo Indians began as soon as each of the twin's eyes could distinguish color and form. The occurrence of *ka-witc*, or twins, was rare and elicited considerable interest among the local natives, for they were traditionally put to death by the northern Pomo. It was thought by the Indians that twinning was caused by the evil wishes of an enemy and that, if the children were allowed to live, they would harm each other. The Pomo culture varied considerably from area to area, with customs and languages that were quite different from place to place even within Potter Valley. For some of the Indians, the attitude towards twins was not necessarily so morbid—rather, curiosity generally prevailed, especially when the twins in question were *ma-san*, or white.

During the period between 1860 and 1865, while Helen Carpenter was busy educating the youngsters of the lower district of Potter Valley, the twins' father, Aurelius, or "Reel," had divided his time between the farm and his interests in the newspaper business. Because journalistic work was not yet available in the small valley, Reel found it necessary to spend much of his time away from home. In 1860, he assisted in the founding of the first newspaper in Ukiah, the *Herald*, published by E. R. Budd. A. O. Carpenter purchased an interest in the enterprise by the spring of 1862. His involvement was short-lived, however, for he sold out to his partner in 1864, traveled to San Francisco, and entered the employment of Dewey and Company. He was hired in the position of foreman of the office of the Mining and Scientific Press.

Arrival of his twin offspring in early 1865 prompted his return to residence in Mendocino County. Because Reel seldom entertained a single interest and fate soon brought him an unexpected appointment as United States Assistant Assessor for the Revenue Department, he journeyed southward once again to accept the post. He was sworn to his duties in Santa Rosa on April 13, 1865, the same day that word reached the area regarding the fall of Richmond. News of Lincoln's assassination followed the next week.

Staging northward to Cloverdale from Santa Rosa, Carpenter was faced with the choice of waiting three days for another stagecoach to Ukiah or seeking another mode of transportation. Having come almost all the way from Kansas by so-called "walker's train," he found foot travel the quickest way over the generally bad roads. It was certainly an easier passage than riding a short distance only to pack a rail beneath the stuck wheels of the stagecoach in order to free it from the axle-deep mud, as was often necessary between Santa Rosa and Cloverdale.

Grace and Grant Carpenter, ca. 1870

Despite the delay that foot travel must have caused, Reel arrived in Ukiah with the first news of the South's defeat, two full days ahead of the mail. He assumed the duties of his new office, first as an assistant assessor and later as deputy collector.

Reel Carpenter found time between his official duties to improve his two farms and registered his Potter Valley property with the General Land Office in San Francisco in July, 1865. His days often extended from sunrise to sunset, filled in the spring with planting and in the autumn with harvest. He hauled pickets for fencing 18 miles with his team of horses, sometimes sleeping overnight beneath the loaded wagon. Back at his property, he drove the fence posts throughout the driving rains of winter. Meanwhile, Helen and his daughter May nursed infant Grace and Grant through their first years of childhood.

Potter Valley remained the family home until 1869. Then, with some hesitation, the Carpenter family pulled up stakes and moved to Ukiah, mostly because of Reel's expanding business activities. Because they felt a great kinship with their first home in Mendocino County, they often returned to the region for pioneer reunions and never quite gave up their ties. Both Grant and young Grace, although just four years old at the time of the move, enjoyed childhood memories of playing in the fields of wild poppies, dashing in and out of creeks, and attending Potter Valley's annual Fourth of July celebrations.

The Carpenter home and studio, Ukiah, ca. 1870

A short time after they had become settled in their new home, the last of the family's four children was born. Frank L. Carpenter joined his two sisters and single brother on November 8, 1870. The Carpenters built a residence and photographic gallery on a downtown thoroughfare at the corner of East Clay and State streets. During the decade that followed, A. O. Carpenter served as Mendocino County deputy assessor, recorder, and road overseer. In the region, however, he is best remembered for his considerable talent with a camera. His photographic business blossomed and grew, evidenced by the many pictures bearing the Carpenter Studio embossure included in albums of the pioneers of the region. Inserts appeared frequently in the personal columns of the *Ukiah City Press* referring to the "picture man."

Carpenter respectfully requests people to pay their bill in order to replenish his stock for the fall season.

or:

Carpenter takes photographic gems for two dollars per dozen.

Despite his success behind a lens, the challenge of the newspaper business in a large town intrigued Reel, even though many aspects of that life were not as appealing to him as his quiet existence in Potter Valley or Ukiah. During August and September, from 1876 to 1878, Reel returned once again to San Francisco and the firm of Dewey and Company to manage, edit, and publish the *Daily Fair* for the Industrial Exhibition Fair of the Mechanic's Institute.

He wrote many letters home describing his busy daily routine—one which left hardly a moment to think.

. . . Dewey stood on his hind legs and howled today when he found that we took proof but once on each article. He said he wanted revises taken after the proofs were corrected . . . It takes two of us to set the ads, make up, take proofs, and give instructions to the typesetters in deciphering the hieroglyphics of the writers.

14

For several years, Reel was in a constant turmoil of indecision between rural or urban living. He wrote to Helen from San Francisco:

I don't expect to stay here. If I took any kind of position, it would involve every day of the week except Sunday and I don't believe we would be a cent better off at the end of the year. I should have to apply myself very closely to make up in time what I lack in speed to do myself credit. If you were here, it might look different, but I am terribly tired of it all.

There was always the invitation for Helen to join him. A few special hints regarding the latest fashions in the city, or a remark or two about his concern for her comfort on her journey to meet him and the possible accommodations for her stay were included. Reel's letters would usually conclude with a line regarding his latest problem or a description of his diet.

As Frank, Grant, and Grace grew older, Reel was not the only Carpenter who traveled about. On several occasions, Helen journeyed to the coast or to the city. As was the custom because of the length of the trip and mode of travel, she usually stayed several days or weeks. In Helen's absence, Carpenter's letters to her often contained descriptions of his worries over the domestic scene at home, the business of the gallery, or more comments intended to entice Helen to cut short her trip and return home a little sooner than planned.

By spring of 1876, Frank was old enough to become a traveling companion for his mother, and the twosome left on an extended trip to southern California that both enabled Frank to see a few of the natural wonders of the area and allowed Helen to visit her family and friends. Neither Grant nor Grace were included because of their involvement in grade school studies in Ukiah. May, who was now 18 years of age, had left home and was attending boarding school classes in the San Francisco bay area.

For a time, Reel was busy at home with his many civic duties, as well as the photographic studio. Then, in a letter to Helen written less than two weeks after her departure, he expresses his loneliness for her:

The Carpenter Family in 1873

I long for you to come home and it seems a year since you left, but, still, I must wait patiently a couple of months. Tell Frank he must be prepared to tell me all he has seen when you get home.

Helen's letters home were mostly descriptive; frequently, however, they omitted the slightest personal comments and eventually brought a stern reprimand from Reel:

You do not say one word of how you are feeling physically or whether you are enjoying yourself, nor do you mention where to write you . . . . There—now make amends in your next letter.

Despite the conflict that Reel Carpenter felt about city life and its excitement, he eventually returned to Ukiah to stay. In 1877, Reel was elected the first marshal of the city, but he declined to run for re-election the following year. Grace and Grant had completed that part of their education offered in rural Ukiah. Even though May had been sent away to continue her education in San Francisco, the decision for the next two offspring to follow her was a parental choice, that depended not only on the consideration of expense, but also on the children's safety and well-being during such an absence. The only mode of transportation to San Francisco was by stagecoach, and the mountainous terrain offered both mud that was often

axle-deep in winter and narrow roads along mountainsides so steep that a stage might tumble several hundred feet before coming to rest at the bottom of some rocky canyon. Highwaymen, such as the notorious Black Bart, lurked around the next bend to relieve passengers of their valuables. Even so, none of these dangers were new nor unusual to members of the well-traveled Carpenter family. In the fall of 1878, Grace left for Normal School in San Francisco while Grant enrolled in the Litton Academy for young men located more closely in nearby Healdsburg.

The attic of the Carpenter dwelling, the Sun House, disclosed in later years an interesting collection of family correspondence from the time that the children were away to school. Several of these letters, written to Grace in San Francisco by Helen, illustrate that the worries and concerns which parents hold regarding their children away from home for the first time have changed very little through the intervening generations.

Dear Gracie:

I am tired but will drop you a line for fear you may be homesick. Your long letter came safely to our hands yesterday. It was first class except for your lack of attention to your orthography [spelling].

We were pleased that you have found a girl that you know. I knew it would not take long for you to become acquainted. Do you ride to and from school all the time?

Do not omit having your window open a little for ventilation. If you should stay one night in a small room with the door and window closed you would be running a risk of making yourself sick. Do not neglect it. Open your window at the top if you are afraid to have it open at the bottom. And if it will not open at the top, ask someone to open it for you. You know, without your health, you can do nothing and small things are sometimes of great importance.

In Annie's letter you speak of staying until five. Do not put in too many hours; it is not good to confine yourself too closely. As soon as your Father told me Old Hughes was by you, I told him the tobacco smell would probably make you sick.

I will send you the paper and it will give you the news. I can think of nothing more. Write whenever you feel like it. We will always be glad to hear from you. You write such nice long letters.

Love and Affection,
Mother

. . . . .

Three decades had passed since the discovery of gold in California, and San Francisco had already become a cultural center of the West. Grace Carpenter found herself in a booming city that many called the "Paris of the West." The new rich, the gold and silver barons, were demanding fine art to adorn their grand mansions atop the peak of Nob Hill.

From around the nation and world, artists flocked to join numerous successful painters and sculptors who had ventured west with the Gold Rush. The San Francisco Art Association had been organized in March, 1871 and formed the first grouping of artists of consequence west of the Mississippi. By 1873, the Association added to its expanding operation the California School of Design, and provided a full schedule of art instruction. It was to this school that Grace Carpenter was drawn, after two years in the Normal School, to begin her study of art. The year was 1879. Virgil Williams was the director of the school, Raymond Yelland instructed landscape classes, and portraiture was taught by Domenico Tojetti.

After her first few months of study, it became obvious that Grace, even at 15, possessed considerable talent. As she left for summer vacation, there evidently was some question regarding her return for further studies in the fall. Oscar Kunath wrote with concern to Grace's mother:

Dear Lady:

As your daughter, Miss Carpenter, is about to return home for the summer, I wish to take the liberty as well as the pleasure in stating that she has been one of my best pupils. The progress I perceived in her work under my direction is surprising and I must confess that she has much talent for artistic drawing; consequently, it would be very unadvisable to exclude her from studies for any length of time. If she intends choosing art for her occupation, it is indeed necessary to devote all her time and talent to this high aim in life. We have hundreds of Lady Artists who never have attained the truly artistic education. Your daughter, being young and possessing such ability, will soon rise above her classmates by studying very earnestly. Hoping, dear lady, that my advice will not be misunderstood, I am yours very

Respectfully,
Osc. Kunath

Grace's parents both realized the fulfillment that education can bring, for Grace was enrolled once again for the fall term at the School of Design.

As Grace returned to school from Ukiah, the slight-figured, sandy-blonde girl quickly distinguished herself from her classmates. Rapidly expanding on her developing skills with both sketch pad and brushes, she filled her easel with anatomical drawings, figure studies of details of the human body, and fledgling landscapes in watercolor. Besides her artwork prepared for classes, Grace also aided her father's photographic business in Ukiah by hand-coloring portraits of prominent citizens.

Communications from her father were spotty. Although Reel was capable of lively correspondence to Helen when the two were separated, writing to his children was rare. Accomplished only at Helen's prodding, the occasion of Grace's sixteenth birthday induced Carpenter to take his pen in hand:

Dear Gracie:

Your mother called me from petting the calf especially to write you for a birthday present. I haven't a thing to write about in the way of news and you know I am not at all on the sentimental lay out.

I want you to be sure and get Chestnut's mother's pictures done as soon as possible and the other one you can be more leisurely about.

I presume you will not forget to add another year to your calendar tomorrow. It seems to me that you have been 15 for several years.

Don't you think Edward and Henry are both coming just a little too often for your own good and theirs? You are two young girls away from home and ought not to receive gent's company too much, not at late hours. Turn them out at 9:30 at the latest.

Be a good girl and never let yourself for a moment forget that your welfare and happiness are as dear to us as life itself. If we do chide you, it is not for selfish motives or mere compliments. Love to you dear one and your big sister.

Father

By the end of the first term of her second year at the School of Design, Grace's diligence at her art studies was rewarded beyond her expectations. The following article appeared in the *Ukiah CityPress* during her vacation at home for Christmas:

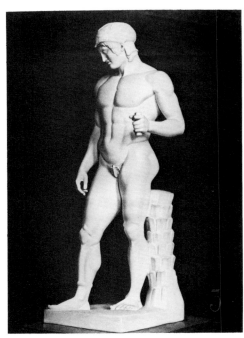

The drawing of Achilles for which Grace Carpenter received the Alvord Gold Medal in 1881.

Last Saturday Miss Grace Carpenter, age sixteen received by telegram the news that she had been awarded the Alvord Gold Medal presented by the President of the San Francisco Art Association for the best full-length study in crayon from a cast at the School of Design. The young lady had returned from the school last week without an idea of the honor that awaited her. That she had succeeded is sufficient proof of the ability and industry she possesses. She is young in both years and experience. She has been a pupil of the art school 18 months and has captured a prize for which others have striven vainly after years of study at the same school. The medal is the object of much solicitude among the students. Ten contestants are selected from among the best students. Six are chosen by the faculty and four by lot. The subject is then assigned. In this instance the subject was Achilles, considered the most difficult in the collection. (The French government under M. Thiers, in gratitude for the nearly $300,000 subscribed by San Franciscans for the relief of French wounded in the Franco-Prussian War, made a gift of a fine collection of classic plaster casts to the Art Association for use in its School of Design.) The competing ten have places assigned and are given one month's time to complete their work on a canvas 2 by 3 feet. The judges are five in number; three being artists and two gentlemen of culture. We cannot doubt Miss Grace deserves the trophy and we are equally sure she will win and worthily wear distinction in her chosen profession. She will resume her studies with the January term of the school.

Both the winning drawing of Achilles and the Carpenter Alvord Gold Medal now rest in the collection of the California Historical Society of San Francisco, a donation by the Carpenter family.

The School of Design was, by the time of Grace's award, in its eighth year of classes and boasted an attendance of 80 pupils. Minutes of the sponsoring Art Association board of directors in the spring of the next year described the school:

The last year of the school has been the most successful since its organization. The class average throughout the year was 79 pupils and the application, improvement and ability shown by them has attracted general remarks.

The landscape class is a distinctive feature of this school. There is no other school in the United States or in Europe that we are aware of that the pupils are taken out by the teachers to make studies of landscapes directly from nature. The usual method being to make copies from lithographs by eminent artists. The improvement arising from these weekly excursions entitles the director of the school to much praise and I have the assurance of some of the pupils that no study of Art could advance them more than this field work.

The late months of 1881 brought celebration of two events to the Carpenter's Ukiah home. On Christmas day, just 25 years before, Aurelius Ormando Carpenter had taken as his bride Helen McCowen, at Prairie City, Kansas. The following May, they had embarked westward in search of the new life that had so richly rewarded them in California. In the holidays of Christmas, 1881, the family also celebrated the announcement of the engagement of their eldest daughter, May. On January 17, 1882, she was married to John Ellis, a former resident of Mendocino County. The *Ukiah City Press* described the occasion:

On Tuesday evening of January 17, 1882, Mr. and Mrs. A. O. Carpenter entertained a houseful of guests for the auspicious occasion of their daughter's marriage. The groom, Mr. John E. Ellis, was formerly a resident of Mendocino and at one time was employed by the Ukiah gas works. At the present time he is superintend-

ent of the Nevada Copper Mining Company at Spenceville in Nevada County.

The house was decorated for the wedding and was thronged with friends of the family . . . They assembled in the parlor at 8:00 o'clock and the Rev. H. B. McBride performed the ceremony after the prescribed form of the Episcopal Church. The paternal Carpenter gave the bride away. Congratulation followed and the ladies were given an opportunity to note the bridal raiment which was rich and handsome . . . The newly married pair will make their home in Spenceville, may it be a happy one.

By 1883, Grace Carpenter had matured into a lovely, graceful, young woman and soon found herself the subject of several gentlemen admirers. Like her sister May, romance found a way into her life. The man of Grace's affection was William T. Davis. There were more than the usual problems of parental approval of a first love, for Davis was 33 years old and produced in Helen and Reel an immediate unfavorable response. With a growing assertion of youthful independence, Grace persisted in the relationship.

When the call of being a grandmother took Helen Carpenter to Spenceville on September 21, 1883, she voiced her opinion of William Davis in a letter written to her daughter, Grace:

I wrote to you last night but have just received your letter. First and foremost, I do not want you to come up here with Davis. Why? For a number of reasons and I know so well what you would say and how you would argue. I do not think it necessary to give any reason at all, but if you have any regards for my wishes you will stay at home. I shall not mention it to May, as I do not wish them to know you would think of such a thing. As for money, I have none to send you . . . none for myself except for $1.20.

I do not know how much longer I will stay. I want to be home in a week or ten days if I can. I do not expect to stop in the city any longer than I have to. Nothing to stop for, only to see you. I guess we will have to postpone our visiting until your vacation.

May received your letter. Davis wrote nothing that required an answer. May is feeling somewhat better today.

The same month, her father wrote that he had no particular objections to William Davis that he could state, only that he considered him to be of "course stock." He continued, "I prefer Edward, but I suppose I shall have to bow to your preference in the matter."

For a time, the question of William Davis was set aside. During the late summer and early autumn of 1883, the senior Carpenters traveled through the countryside of Mendocino Country photographing the residents of each mountain community. *The Mendocino Democrat* commented, on August 24, 1883:

A. O. Carpenter and wife are camping at Covelo in Round Valley and while there, Mr. Carpenter is employing his time taking pictures.

When Reel and Helen returned home, they sent Grace a number of portraits to photochrome—hand color in light oil paints. Most such photographs, striking eye-catchers in a day before color photography had become practical, were to be used as objects of display in well-traveled businesses and home parlors.

The holiday period between school terms brought Grace home to participate in the festivities. She seemed to love dancing and seldom missed an occasion to "kick up her heels." On Friday evening of January 4, 1884, the first Leap Year

Ball was held in Ukiah by the young ladies of the town. As was the custom of the day, Grace's dance program was filled with the eligible young men of the town for all 24 listings. The evening began with a Grand March, followed by a mixture of waltzes, quadrilles, and hops.

Following the holidays, Grace returned to the School of Design for what is believed to have been her last term. With her attendance in the spring session of 1884, she had completed her formal art training. Only a few sketch pads and an anatomy lesson book have remained in the family collection of the period, and few examples are known to reveal her developing talent. It was not until 1890 that Grace began keeping complete and accurate records of her progress.

During the following summer, Grace visited family friends in Lakeport. She occupied her time with many of the same pastimes that other 19-year old girls of the period enjoyed, including a great deal of horseback riding. In addition, however, Grace also utilized her first truely free summer to sketch scenes in the Clear Lake area.

Grace Carpenter's love for William Davis had not been dimmed by the long summer of the coast-range valleys. By now, the family referred to him only when absolutely necessary. Then, on September 17, 1884, in what amounted to an elopement, Grace and Davis were married in San Francisco. She was just 19. Announcement of the event in the Ukiah newspaper was limited to the vital statistics column.

The Carpenter's reaction to the marriage is unrecorded, but doubtless was one of disappointment. In later years, the subject of Grace's union with Davis was never mentioned among friends or relatives, and speculation regarding their relationship must, of necessity, be left for the pen of the fiction writer. Every avenue of research on the matter has proven fruitless.

On December 16, 1885, William Davis and Grace were divorced. The effect of the unhappiness of those 15 months on the young artist's creative ability was profound; rare is the signature of Grace Carpenter Davis found on paintings. A few, however, do exist, and there may be others as yet unrecognized. For a long period of time, her creative talents were stilled.

It may be assumed that the Davises were separated before their divorce was granted. Laws of the period required a 12-month waiting period for a dissolution of marriage. During at least part of the time, she resided in Ukiah and photochromed photographic portraits in her father's gallery.

On September 19, 1884, her twin brother Grant left for Ann Arbor, Michigan, where he began a course of study in law at the University of Michigan. In the interim between Grace's marriage to Davis and her subsequent divorce, the Carpenter family had been consumed with activity. With the meridian of life approaching for Helen and Reel, A. O. Carpenter decided to place his hat in the election ring and seek the office of City Treasurer. Although the office was non-partisan, a victory for a "Black Republican" like Reel in the heavily-Democratic area would have been an accomplishment indeed. He instead was soundly defeated. One small victory in his loss could not be passed over by the local journalists, however. His opponent, also a photographer, found it necessary to close his studio to assume his position as City Treasurer.

The stigma of divorce in a small 1880's community had no exception in Ukiah. More than two years passed from the end of her marriage to William Davis before Grace felt that fun and parties had eluded her long enough. In the holiday season of 1887, she hosted many of her friends and acquaintances to a party. The *Ukiah City Press* described the event:

One of the most original, unique, grotesque, and enjoyable entertainments ever

20

witnessed in Ukiah was the party given by Mrs. Grace Davis at her cozy little studio on Main Street, Tuesday evening.

Early in the day, her brother, Master Frank Carpenter, notified a chosen number of friends and acquaintances that the pleasure of their company was requested at the studio in the evening. It was intimated that no one would be considered in full dress who did not give evidence of an unsound mind by their costume. We were honored by being among the "elect." Though not wishing to be sent to Napa [a nearby mental institution], the merry twinkle in the young man's eye and the well-known reputation of the fair hostess for mirth was too much for our "weak mind," and choosing our everyday girl, we, "two loving hearts which beat as one," hastened to the studio of the artist. The location was marked by a number of tastefully arranged Chinese lanterns, which some of the "crazy boys" soon found time to hang on a tree on the opposite side of the street. Within were gathered half a hundred of the merriest of the good people of the town, who needed nothing but the inquisition of our Superior Judge to make them fit subjects for the asylum, if their subsequent actions were to be put in evidence. It was indeed a crazy party, for all sense of the world's cares was lost in the revelry of innocent pleasure. After a luncheon of most excellent tea and cakes, the evening was devoted to music, ala silver band, and games. It was not until near midnight that the happy troupe remembered that sleep is necessary for the human body. A unanimous vote of thanks was silently tendered the originator of the idea of a "crazy party," and all decided more such entertainments should be given.

Grace Carpenter was now 22 years old. A popular member of Ukiah's social life, her youth had been filled with the frontier town, countryside, and its people. To her background in art, Grace had added a growing maturity that had been tempered by her marriage to William Davis. She stood at the threshold of a notable career.

CHAPTER 2

THE BUDDING CAREER

An Enduring, Second Marriage and a First Major Work

HORACE GREELEY'S admonition of 1851, "Go West, young man," was still sound advice in 1889. In spring of that year, John Wilz Napier Hudson, M. D., arrived in Ukiah. He had traveled all the way from Nashville, Tennessee to practice medicine in the quiet little valley communities of northern California's coast mountain range. The town welcomed him with open arms, and he established an office in downtown Ukiah, near Standley Street. Seeking room and board with the South Methodist Church pastor's family until August, he finally settled in the popular Palace Hotel.

John Wilz Napier Hudson

The news quickly spread that a tall, dark, and handsome young bachelor had arrived in town. For those young ladies enjoying poor health, the problem of introduction offered little inconvenience. The remainder of the town's eligible ladies contented themselves with the hope that he would soon attend a forthcoming social event. Such an opportunity soon arose. April saw the inauguration of the first annual ball of the Native Sons of the Golden West. Evidently, insufficient "native sons" were available to fill the dance programs of the daughters, for the newcomer was invited to the festivities.

It was reported in the *Ukiah City Press*:

The hall never looked so well. The decorations were fastidious and beautiful, as well as appropriate. From the front of the stage was suspended a huge bear, emblematic of the order. The programs were elaborate and were only equalled by the elegant invitations issued some two weeks previous. The music was excellent and combined with the brilliant gas jets, the warbling of birds suspended from masses of evergreen, the delicate perfume of flowers and the handsome toilets of the ladies produced the most exquisite atmosphere. Among the young ladies who participated in the dance was Mrs. Grace Davis, wearing a brown princess gown with a sash . . .

Love and courtship may well have begun between Grace Davis and the handsome John Hudson at that very ball. In the weeks and months which followed, the couple became a familiar sight around the streets of Ukiah.

Dr. Hudson quickly won the confidence of his patients and the community. On June 28, 1889, he received the appointment to physician and surgeon for the San Francisco and North Pacific Railroad Company, with residence in Ukiah. It was considered an excellent appointment and was one which he deserved.

On October 7, 1889, Grace opened her art studio to the public and busied herself giving art lessons. In addition to an assortment of beautiful paintings, it contained a valuable collection of curios. She also began exhibiting her artwork locally. The seventh annual fair in Ukiah, held in October of 1889, awarded Grace honors for an oil portrait, an oil landscape, a pen drawing, for the largest collection of paintings, and for, curiously, taxidermy.

Busy as both Grace and John were, they found time to fall in love. On April 29, 1890, just 13 months after his arrival in Ukiah, the couple was married. The social column of the *Ukiah City Press* reported the nuptials of the Hudsons more extensively than those which had accompanied Grace's first marriage to William Davis, some six years earlier:

John and Grace Carpenter Hudson,
August 1890

> The wedding which took place Wednesday evening at the residence of Mr. and Mrs. A. O. Carpenter was a pretty and a delightful affair and only witnessed by their relatives and the contracting parties.
>
> The occasion was the marriage of their daughter, Grace Carpenter Davis, a most brilliant and accomplished lady, as we all know, to Dr. J. W. Hudson, a promising physician of this place, lately from the South.
>
> To the inspiring strains of the Wedding March, executed by Mrs. A. D. McMillian, the party entered as follows: Dr. Hudson and Mrs. Joseph Thomas, Mrs. A. O. Carpenter, the mother of the bride, escorted by her son, Frank, followed by the bride leaning on the arm of her father, Mr. A. O. Carpenter.
>
> The bridal party took their places amongst garlands of smilax, maidenhair fern, bridal wreath, and the choicest of delicate white blossoms, and the ceremony was performed by Rev. Harrison Price in the rites of the Episcopal ceremony, after his usual impressive and solemn way. Then followed by the congratulations of all present, in the heartiest manner, wishing the newly wedded pair all the good things that are allowed to mortals.
>
> The ceremony was immediately followed by the wedding banquet, which was sumtuous in every respect and greatly enjoyed amid the bright sayings and general, witty conversation of the entire party.
>
> At the tables the floral decorations were particularly noticable. The sweetest and most beautiful roses and lilies in every tint were in tasteful profusion.
>
> Among the gifts were many rare and beautiful tributes. From every direction they showed the esteem in which the young couple are held by their numerous friends and relatives. Many of the bride's friends considered flowers the most fitting tribute to her. She was generously remembered from here and abroad. The guests numbered only a little over 20, for, as we have said, only relatives were in attendance. The official witnesses were Sam D. Paxton, Hale McCowen, and Joseph M. Thomas.

For a short time the newlyweds lived with Grace's parents, until a convenient addition could be made to Grace's modest studio on the north side of West Clay Street.

Until this time, Grace had not directed her artistic talents in a specific direction. Few examples of her work before 1890 remain, other than art school sketch pads and occasional paintings that were done more for experience than for any serious purpose. The avenues she explored, like those followed by any accomplished artist, included various subjects—landscapes, portraits, still life, sketches—as well as other media—watercolors, crayons, pen and ink.

In time, Grace Hudson settled on both a theme and a style that were to remain remarkably consistent throughout her professional life. Portraying the Pomo Indians became her goal, one which set her apart as an artist. Without question, Grace Hudson painted Indian life more true to reality than any of her contemporaries. What began as an aid to further her husband's interest in archeology and

24

ethnology, evolved into a fulltime occupation. Together, the contribution of Grace and John Hudson was a remarkable effort to perserve the history of a vanishing race of people.

Genius without originality is commonplace and the path which Grace followed in committing the Pomos to canvas made her unique. Her first attempt at portraying a Pomo infant was typical of the style that brought her recognition and fame as an artist throughout the remainder of her life. For the first time, she raised her brush with the certainty of thought and awareness of firm intent. She was just 26 years of age, and the result of her effort was notable.

The *Dispatch Democrat*, a Ukiah local paper, carried the following article on July 3, 1891:

We had the pleasure last Saturday of visiting the studio of Mrs. Dr. Hudson. The principle object of our visit was to view the painting which this lady has about completed for the Minneapolis Art Association, which is the leading institution of its kind in America, and which has brought to this country the most-noted works of the old masters. The painting represents the papoose of Whisky Jennie, one of Pinoleville's dusky matrons, tied up in an Indian baby basket. The mother has put the baby to sleep and stood the basket up against a tree, and put her dog beside it to keep watch. The subject is a most interesting one and has been handled with a master's touch.

H. J. Smith, the art collector of the association referred to above, recently visited Mrs. Hudson's studio, when the painting was yet in an unfinished state, and he was so favorably impressed with it that he immediately ordered it for the association he represented. It is now finished and will be shipped to Minneapolis next week.

As the Minneapolis Art Association handles nothing but the very highest class of art, the compliment which has been paid Mrs. Hudson is a very high one, and it is testimonial to her ability that she, as well as all of our people, should be proud of.

National Thorn
Location Unknown

The reasons surrounding H. Jay Smith's visit to Ukiah in the summer of 1891 remain a mystery; it was one of those events that marked a turning point in the life of young Grace.

By October 2, 1891, the news had returned to Ukiah of "A Flattering Compliment." Palmer Henderson, the art critic of the *Minneapolis Journal*, in his "Exposition Art Notes," had the following to say of the new painting by Grace Hudson:

Did you ever see anything cuter than that little Indian baby asleep on his cradleboard? It was painted by Mrs. Hudson of California from life. 'Tis the papoose of a woman from whom Mr. Smith, of the Minneapolis Art Association, bought a number of his Indian baskets. The little fellow is chubby, and warm from sleeping and the heavy blanket in which he is bundled. The flesh is very good; one can almost feel it.

He is securely fastened to the basket-like sides by rope laced across through the loops. From it, above, dangles a string of beads, evidently to break the tedium of his waking hours. Upon the ground is spread the bright plaid showl, which is probably envied by every other woman in the tribe, and an alert terrier guards the slumber of the little one. It is a good painting and popular picture.

When it was considered that the painting of Ukiah's gifted woman artist was added to one of the major Midwestern collections of the time, and that it was among the few singled for special notice by the critics, the honor and compliment paid Grace Hudson did not go unnoticed by her fellow townsfolk.

Grace entitled the painting *National Thorn* and numbered it "1." The 30- by 30-inch painting was the first in a series of 684 numbered paintings completed during her lifetime.

The strict self-discipline that was to develop later was not evident in these early years. Her honeymoon was not yet over, and the beautiful weather and magnificent scenery of what was to become California's premiere wine district were not conducive to her confinement in a studio. She had art students to teach, as well as preparations to make for becoming superintendent of the drawing-room work for the local Methodist Church. Nor was oil painting her only artistic outlet. Grace prepared entries for fairs, taking awards for a hearth rug and for her silk patchwork, as well as for her oils and watercolors.

The doctor and she took buggy rides, picnicking on the banks of the Russian River at well-known Pieta Creek. On other occasions, they walked along the river to discover budding pussywillows and hiked up Mill Creek to see the ferns and star-shaped Easter lilies. Sometimes they walked through valley meadows to glimpse quail quickly running for cover and watched the flight of doves from their feeding grounds. The beauty of nature was all about them, but Grace was in no hurry to capture it with paint and brush.

MAJOR ACHIEVEMENTS

Little Mendocino and the World's Fair

BUILDING ON THE REPUTATION that her first numbered canvas had helped to bring, Grace Hudson painted several important portraits during 1892 and 1893. They traveled the expanse of the United States and hung in exhibits of the San Francisco Art Association, the Mechanics Fair in San Francisco, Minneapolis Exposition, Columbian Exposition in Chicago, and other galleries. One painting found a permanent home in the Smithsonian Institution. During the period, Grace also gained recognition as a magazine illustrator.

Her first portrait painted after the overwhelming response to *National Thorn* was titled *Belle of the Tribe*, and numbered "2." Its subject was an Indian girl named Katum, and the canvas was one of the few portraits which remained in the family collection during the lifetime of the artist. It was rediscovered in the attic of the Carpenter's "Sun House" in 1968.

Two articles appeared following the completion of *Belle of the Tribe*, both of which described the viewer's response to the intricate detail and striking composition of the painting. The first of these articles appeared in *Frank Leslie's Popular Monthly* in April, 1897:

Belle of the Tribe (Katum)
Private Collection

. . . but the Belle of Pinoleville is undoubtedly Katum, in whose dusky beauty can be traced a touch of white blood. Mrs. Hudson painted her with a wealth of hair unbound and streaming over a voluptuous form, the curves of which are lost in a deerskin jacket. The coloring is sumptuous; and it would be hard to surpass the sky glory of the eyes and the tender, living warmth with which the head is imbued. So beautiful is the face that there crept into my mind a suspicion of fantasy on the part of the artist. This was only dispelled by the presence one day in the studio of Katum herself. Realization was forced home to stay that, however idealistic is Mrs. Hudson's own nature, she never idealizes her subject. Her respect for human features is such that she takes no liberties with their delineation.

A review in the *Illustrated Pacific States*, September, 1894, followed:

In this brief sketch we can mention but a few of her paintings, yet the following are among those which have won marked attention from the critics and have received the admiration of thousands: The Belle of the Tribe, *showing the head of a young Indian girl is Mrs. Hudson's own favorite of her creations. The dark, wild beauty of nature's own unlettered daughter and the uncurbed, passionate spirit, her inheritance from the boundless freedom that surrounds her, are delineated with rare power. But there is a realistic touch, a suggestion of the coarse, of the natural, coming over the rounded lines and emboldening the shy glory of the eyes which gives this painting the value of being a true mirror of reality, instead of the fanciful, if beautiful, conceptions which exist rarely but in the ideal.*

During spring and autumn of 1892, Katum's portrait appeared in the San Francisco Art Association exhibit and at the Minneapolis Exposition throughout the following summer.

Her third numbered work was of a Pomo Indian chief, Captain John Mewhinney. Grace had, of course, spent her entire youth with Captain John's presence and likely knew his features as well as those of any Indian in Potter Valley. An article by Ninetta Eames, which appeared in *Frank Leslie's Popular Monthly* of April, 1897, and which the above reference to Katum shared, commented regarding Grace Hudson, her subject, and the painting:

. . . With a whole rancheria at hand, she wins her dusky subjects to sit for her by a variety of adroit devices which mark her a born tactician as well as one thoroughly at home with Indian idiosyncracies. Nor is this to be wondered at. "Captain John," the aged chief of a pitiful remnant of the Yo-ki-os, has known her all his life. When admitting the fact, he adds, with a humorous twinkle in his almost sightless eyes, "Grace my folks!" She vividly recalls how he appeared to her childish eyes—a muscular figure wrapped in a dingy blanket, above whose fold was thrust his big shaggy head. There was nothing terrifying about him; quite the reverse, in fact, for he could be very funny. She and her sister and two brothers used to laugh at him until their sides ached, for he was a born comedian . . . Captain John would get down on all fours and go through the spirited pantomime of a bucking horse, or play he was fighting a grizzly, that he might lead the children up to an awestruck study of the deep scars on his arms and breast, the result of actual conflict with Ursus Horribilis.

He is yet a jolly old heathen, this native centenarian, and takes a child-like pride in a life-size painting of himself, to which he says, with a carefree laugh, "By-'n-by, Cap'n John die. My frens say, 'John no die. Here Cap'n John!' "

This picture of the chief was the first to emphasize the genius of the young artist. A traveling art dealer for an Eastern firm happened into her studio one day, while the venerable sitter was shifting his position uneasily before the painter's eager eyes. The hand guiding the brush moved swiftly, but with a relentless observance of the minutia that set lines about her firm pretty mouth. The stranger was instantly struck by the wonderful transference of expression to the big, seamy face on the canvas, and the unflinching honesty that omitted not the finest wrinkle or a single bristle that adorned the rugged chin and head. Even the elaborate barbarity of the dress—a rabbit-skin robe held in place by a long wooden pin—was brought out with faultless precision.

Immediately a price was offered for the picture that, as Mrs. Hudson afterward expressed it, "Fairly took my breath away, it seemed so munificent;" and forthwith Captain John was packed and sent across the continent, where it occupies a place of honor in a metropolitan gallery.

Captain John Mewhinney
Private Collection

Grace's portrait of Captain John is today the possession of the National Collection of Fine Arts, in Washington, D. C. Mrs. Hudson made a copy of the work, perhaps for sentimental reasons, which remained in the family collection. As well as can be determined, this was the only occasion when she made a copy of her work, except possibly paintings to replace those destroyed in the catastrophic fire in San Francisco which followed the earthquake of 1906.

From the very beginning, however, Grace Hudson had taken two measures to preserve her recollection of her artwork that today serve as incomparably valuable tools in authenticating and dating her paintings. Besides the numbering system she applied to all works she considered major, she kept a small, tidy notebook with a full description of the painting, its dimensions, date of completion, and its new owner. In addition, she called upon her father's photographic talents to record each of the paintings as it was completed. The combination of these efforts to document her work have provided art historians a unique insight into the progression and development of her style.

Grace's final effort for 1892 was titled *The Interrupted Bath*, and was assigned the number "4." It was exhibited both in August, 1892, at the Minneapolis Exposition, and in the following year at the Columbian Exposition in Chicago. Because Helen Carpenter used the painting to illustrate an article she had written for the *Overland Monthly* which depicted life among the Pomos, the painting also came to be known by the title, *Quail Baby*.

Grace provided more than 70 pen-and-ink illustrations for articles that appeared in *Overland Monthly*. Most of these were written by her close friend, Ninetta Eames, and others. As her author friends sought with pen and paper to convey the atmosphere of northern California's Mendocino County life, Grace's line drawings captured its personalities and environment.

Without exception, each of the paintings completed during 1892 had furthered Grace Carpenter Hudson's reputation and sphere of influence. In a span of a few months from the time that she first sketched studies for *National Thorn*, the art world recognized that her paintings stood unique in the West. Grace found herself on the threshold of national prominence.

The Interrupted Bath (Quail Baby)
Private Collection

. . . . .

Perhaps no other single painting by a California artist has created as much interest in the art world as Grace Hudson's first major canvas of 1893, *Little Mendocino*. Numbered "5," it became a popular attraction at major exhibitions and was hung that winter at the 27th annual Midwinter Fair in San Francisco, popularly-known as the Mechanics Fair. The following year it was exhibited at the Columbian Exposition in Chicago. Throughout the more than eight decades since its completion, it has focused more attention on the artist's work than any other single painting she produced.

On January 23, 1893, the *San Francisco Call* carried an article that referred to *Little Mendocino* as something of a daring subject:

. . . for short of absolute success, it would be ridiculous; but the Indian baby is not ridiculous; it is charming, in spite of the fact that it is crying. Everyone admires the little brown thing and longs to comfort it. Indeed, Mrs. Grace Hudson has scored a distinct success with her well-painted "papoose." It stands out admirably from along view and will also bear the closest inspection. It is distinct and yet soft.

The Ukiah *Republican Press* reported in an article written January 27, 1893:

. . . We are "In it" [the Mechanics Fair] *far better than we know. The crowning glory of the Mendocino exhibit (if we may claim the glory, since the work was done by a Ukiah lady) is Mrs. Hudson's already-famous picture representing a papoose, wrapped in a blanket and securely-tied with strong cords (after the manner of Indian babies in general) in its basket resting against the foliage of a red-*

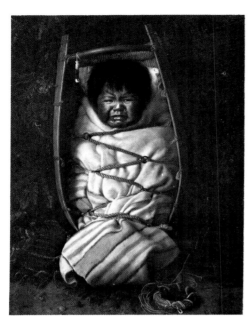

Little Mendocino
Private Collection

wood tree. Its mother has undoubtedly left to gather blackberries or perchance acorns, or to hunt for a savory mess of young yellow jackets, for a tear courses down the dusky face in such a natural way that a lady was heard to remark, "Oh, I feel as though I must wipe that tear from the poor thing's face!"

A fellow exile from Mendocino County longed to pluck a twig of the redwood, as it seemed almost stirred by a gentle Mendocino breeze. It is altogether the most striking picture in the entire collection, the effect being admirable from the opposite side of the gallery, and yet bearing the closest inspection without losing any of the distinctness or soft toning of color.

Connisseurs pronounce it the best painting on exhibition from the novelty of the subject and the excellent execution of the artist. It differs from most of the pictures insomuch that the work is finer, shows well in any light and will stand close scrutiny.

The picture, which had begun the exhibit from a location that was in a remote corner of the gallery of the Mechanic's Fair, attracted so much attention that soon it was moved to a place of honor on the main wall of the gallery.

It was not long before the young lady from northern California was recognized and entertained by the socially elite of the San Francisco bay area.

Mrs. Alexander F. Fisher-Hamilton gave a pleasant tea at her home, 951 Chestnut Street, yesterday afternoon, to show the latest pictures of Miss [sic] Grace Hudson to a few friends. Mrs. Fisher-Hamilton, assisted by the young artist, received the guests. They conversed in the parlors, which were prettily decorated with the paintings. They are, indeed, creditable and were greatly admired. Light refreshments were served during the afternoon. It is Miss [sic] Hudson's intention to send her paintings with the State exhibit to the World's Fair.

As the time approached for *Little Mendocino* to be shipped to Chicago for exhibition there in 1893, a problem arose regarding where the painting would be hung. It was said that the matter created concern by Grace's friends, for they worried that she was heavily burdened by the difficulty.

Mrs. Waite, President of the Women's Auxillary to the National Exhibit at the World's Fair is positively stuck on having at her pretty headquarters Mrs. Hudson's famous painting, Little Mendocino. *And then there is Mrs. Smith, President of the Women's Auxillary to the California Exhibit, whose mind is just as made up to have* Little Mendocino *at her headquarters; and "that settles it," she says, "and the other Mrs. President can just 'Waite' til Columbus is another hundred years older, if she likes."*

Don't you think the situation trying enough to demoralize even the steady-nerved artist of Mendocino? It is said this good lady, who is in the city to remain until the close of the fair, appealed to her husband in Ukiah to know what to do. She received word from the doctor to settle the matter by making a bluff at doing the King Solomon act of severing the painted baby in twain.

Evidently, Mrs. Waite did wait. In the California Building at the World's Columbian Exposition there were at least three rooms under the care of Mrs. Smith and the local ladies, one of which was devoted particularly to literature and art. Called the Eschscholtzia room—after the California poppy, the state flower—it was decorated in gold. In frames supplied by the gallery of Morris and Kennedy, two of Grace Hudson's oils were hung, *Little Mendocino* and *The Interrupted Bath*.

30

Mrs. Hudson's contribution to the show did not pass unnoticed by the *Dispatch and Democrat* back in Ukiah, for on July 6, 1894, the paper noted:

> On Monday last Mrs. Grace Hudson, the well-known artist of this place, received a diploma from the World's Fair management, conferring "honorable mention" on her painting. Coming in competition, as it did, with the greatest paintings of the masters of the world, this honorable mention is a recognition of Mrs. Hudson's work of which she may well feel proud.

Following the fair, the painting of *Little Mendocino* passed into the hands of Col. M. H. Hecht. Today, the painting belongs to the California Historical Society, donated with the late Louis Sloss, Jr. Collection. It has been included in numerous exhibitions besides those previously mentioned, and will likely be a part of other showings of California art for generations yet to come.

On December 8, 1895, however, the painting was nearing the climax of its fame. A news clipping from the *San Francisco Chronicle* of that date described a forgery of the painting that enraged artists and critics throughout the city:

> There is a grievance among the artists of the city over what they regard as unjust treatment of one of their number by a local exhibitor and dealer. Other exhibitors, quite a number of them, seem to think the grievance a just one, and are rather caustic in their criticisms.
>
> There is on exhibition in the windows of a Grant Avenue store a painting entitled Little Mendocino. From a frame of redwood bark, a tear-stained papoose, with face screwed up for weeping, stares at the passerby. At first glance the painting bears a close resemblance to the picture bearing the same title painted by Grace Hudson and now the property of Colonel M. H. Hecht. The imitation of color and treatment is photographic in the minuteness of detail.
>
> The identity of the imitator and how he obtained the opportunity to make a copy of the picture are questions which a number of artists would like to have answered. The dealer knows, but does not care to talk.
>
> Some time ago the original picture, Colonel Hecht's property, was in the same window and bore the price mark of $1,000. The imitation was there at the same time, marked $150. This is regarded by artists as a gross breach of proprieties. Complaint was made, and the original picture no longer graces the show window. The imitation was there yesterday, but it may be removed today, for the dealer has announced his intention of adorning the walls of his own home with the copy of Little Mendocino.
>
> When asked about the trouble yesterday, he had this to say:
>
> "An artist said to me that he could paint just as good a picture of an Indian baby as Mrs. Hudson could. I did not believe it, but I told him he could try, as I wanted to see what he could do.
>
> "There is nothing wrong in copying a picture. It is done in Paris, Munich, Berlin. All the old masters are copied. Besides, we had the copy photographed thinking we could sell the pictures, but they did not sell. I am going to take the picture home. Colonel Hecht is abroad, and knows nothing about the copy having been made."

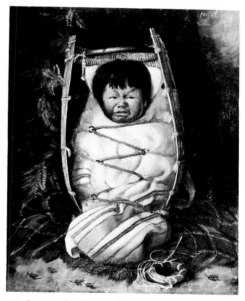

Little Mendocino, Fake

This little newspaper bomb quickly brought a response from the imitator. The following article, titled "Little Mendocino Again," appeared the next week:

> Theophilus Reichard copied it. The clever copy of Grace Hudson's picture, Little Mendocino, *which was exposed in the* Chronicle *and which, by the way,*

was not exhibited at Schussler's, has occasioned much talk above the palettes. It seems that Theophilus Reichard, the Eastern artist, who has only been in San Francisco 18 months, was the man who copied the picture.

Mr. Reichard said yesterday, "Yes, I copied the original which belongs to Colonel Hecht. I also touched up the original for Mr. Hecht. I don't see what all this hue and cry is about. In Europe and the Eastern states all the famous pictures are copied and sold. Rosa Bonheur copies her own pictures and sells them. Sometimes the copies are better than the originals. I can't see that it reflects either on the painter or the artist who copies."

All the publicity, of course, only helped to further bring Grace's painting to the public's attention. It was not long before *Little Mendocino* was gracing novelty counters on picture postcards.

Because of the overwhelming triumph of *Little Mendocino* and an absorbing interest in magazine illustrations, Grace produced a few major paintings in 1893. Even so, 17 numbers were added to her growing notebook by the close of the year.

Paintings "six" through "twelve" were recorded simply as "miniature baby on oval plaque," and pose a broad gap in understanding Grace Hudson's early work. None of the plaques have been located, nor were any photographed or kept otherwise in the family's records. Paintings "13" and "14" were miniature reproductions of *National Thorn* and *Little Mendocino* respectively. Number "15" was likewise a small oil, six by four inches in size, and was titled *Billy Kept Plump*. The homely little painting appeared in an article in *Overland Monthly*.

Mrs. Hudson was gaining a reputation as a portrait artist, but if the subject of her attention called for a pail or a head of cabbage, these details were treated with the same attention as the tremulous eyes of one of her larger canvases, such as *The Quail Baby*. Her next painting, number "15," was a small three-quarter-length panel of Katum, the same Pomo woman featured in *Belle of the Tribe*. Katum, with closely-cropped hair and a peasant blouse, was presented in striking contrast to the refined formal portrait painted the year before. Instead of the mature face of the earlier canvas, she appeared as a youthful coquette, with a sly smile on her face and a beautiful basket held in her hands.

Completing the paintings Grace finished in 1893 was her winter project, number "17." Titled *The Turnip Baby*, it was a major canvas of striking dimensions. At 35½ by 28½ inches, it was even larger than *Little Mendocino*. The *Oakland Tribune* described the new painting in glowing terms:

Turnip Baby
Private Collection

California is the land of sunshine, flowers and romance, and should be the land of art and artists, for these go naturally together. From time to time, one sees in the galleries and art stores excellent examples of work done by our home people. Just now Mrs. Grace Hudson of Ukiah has on exhibition at Morris and Kennedy's galleries on Post Street, San Francisco, one of her characteristic paintings of an Indian papoose. This shows that the artist is making great advancement in her work. The painting, which represents an Indian baby munching a turnip—to which business the youngster is giving his whole little mind—while a rough-and-ready small dog of no particular breed is fully awake and watchful at the papoose's side, is admirably worked out in all its details and is wonderfully realistic. Homely as the subject is, and much as it might be despised by one with less artistic feeling than Mrs. Hudson, the picture is most attractive and pleasing, and one would never tire of looking at it. The baby, with his sullen, Indian eyes, is real, alive and human; and one can readily imagine that even at his early age, and while his only costume is a rope and an old blanket, he would enjoy a scalplock rather than a rattle to play with. The still-life in the picture could hardly be better; in fact, the whole picture is so consciously done in every way, and shows such ar-

32

tistic genius, that it needs no prophet to tell the future of the artist. Those who are familiar with Mrs. Hudson's illustrations in the Overland Monthly *and other publications know that she excels, not only in detail work and as a colorist, but also in her ability to put expression into a face; and someday she will paint a companion piece for Gabriel Max's* Visions, *for she has all of the best years of her life before her and that persistent patience and energy which, when combined with artistic ability, insures success.*

Several feature articles in both newspapers and magazines of the day mentioned that the life-sized portrait of *The Turnip Baby* was purchased by Samuel A. Pond, the ex-mayor of San Francisco. The painting has remained in the Pond family through the years, and one interesting anecdote is still told on occasions of family gatherings regarding Mrs. Hudson's work.

The story of the San Francisco tragedy of 1906 is repeated only to set the scene. The Pond residence was then located atop Nob Hill, where every home was completely destroyed by the fire which consumed much of the city in the wake of the earthquake. Mrs. Pond, confronted with the perplexing question of what material possession was worth risking her life to save, chose *The Turnip Baby* above all else. She hurriedly removed the canvas from the frame and stretcher with a butcher knife, pinning it to her undergarments for safe-keeping before fleeing the residence. There it remained throughout the holocaust.

. . . . .

During the early days of the West, a man was usually judged by his physical strength and endurance rather than by his mental ability. When a man's worth was evaluated, be it for his service to his fellow man or for his attributes as a prospective bridegroom, no greater compliment could be made than that he be called a "hard worker."

Grace Hudson's companion in life, being a physician, was usually exempted from the deliberation of Ukiah's self-appointed jurors, and was instead afforded the respect due a professional man. His marriage into one of the most popular families in the town helped make him an accepted native of the community. Despite his achievements and social position, however, John Hudson soon created a response of mixed emotions, as often was the case when one chose not to fit into the accepted categories of social order in a small town.

Beside his talent and training in the field of medicine, John was drawn to studies of the ethnology and anthropology of the Pomo Indians. He recorded their language, learned their customs, and collected their artifacts.

By 1894, he had gathered a collection of Pomo Indian baskets still believed unequalled. In time, his study of baskets caused him to write an article on the subject for the *Overland Monthly* which has appeared since his time in the bibliography of every book written about the handicraft. His ever-increasing interest in Indian ethnology left little time or inclination for the practice of medicine and, by 1896, his card had been omitted from the front-page column of the *Ukiah City Press*, where it had appeared with the professional listings for more than seven years.

While Dr. Hudson was forging the basis for a common interest that bound he and his wife's marriage for more than 45 years, Grace was capturing the Indians' portraits on canvas. The year of 1894 brought forth eleven canvases from the studio in Ukiah, each of which found their way into exhibits at Macbeth's in New York, Thurber's in Chicago, the Denver Art Club, the Oakland Museum, or the San Francisco Press Club. As Grace put her 30th birthday behind her, she completed illustrations for three more magazine articles.

The first two paintings of the new year, *Lonesome* and *Apple Baby*, numbers "18" and "19" respectively, were small canvases similar in subject to those of earlier years. Both depicted Pomo youngsters. Oftentimes, Hudson paintings were renamed by art dealers, newspaper columnists, and, on occasion, even by gallery audiences. *Lonesome*, for example, was later referred to as *Friends*.

If her first paintings of the year had been small in dimension, *Yokia Treasures*, number "20," was perhaps the largest canvas that Grace Hudson ever painted. With dimensions of 38- by 30-inches, it had an area of a little more than 1000-square inches. Soon after its completion, it was shipped to Macbeth's in New York City, where it was purchased by Mrs. George H. Morrell of Boston. An April, 1894 column in the *San Francisco Chronicle*, accompanied by a rather incomplete sketch and an inaccurate Grace Hudson biography, mentioned the artwork:

Yokia Treasures
Location unknown

. . . *A visit to her pretty studio a short time ago found her at work on a subject rather more ambitious than any she has before undertaken. It is called* Ukiah Treasures [sic].

The treasures are the three things most highly prized by the Indian—his child, his dog and a fancy basket. The child, one of the few still retaining the rich coloring of the old race, stands clad in a short, dirty shirt, munching a cake, while the dog, with pricked ears and body all aquiver with the longing, sits at its feet waiting for the crumbs he fondly hopes may fall to his share. Behind the two is seen one of the wonderful baskets woven by this tribe. The basket is almost as tall as the child, and probably, if the Indian were called upon to part with two of his three treasures, he would keep the basket. This unfinished picture is the only one of her Indian pictures which remains in the possession of the artist.

A few years ago, Miss Carpenter married Dr. Hudson, a young physician from the South, and it is to his intelligent criticism and encouragement that she ascribes the greater part of her success in her chosen field of work. Himself an eager worker among the Indian relics, he is well fitted for the position of critic on all questions regarding the race. Mrs. Hudson's studio is in a little cottage a few blocks from the busy center of Ukiah. The walls of her reception room are completely covered by her collection of curios and relics of the vanishing race which she has chosen to preserve on canvas.

Frequently, Grace Hudson's paintings found their way into the hands of well-known collectors. Grace recorded that *Disappointment*, number "21," was purchased by Leon Sloss, but the canvas has not been found in his collection. Its subject was a crying baby with a broken egg. Just as often, Mrs. Hudson painted pictures as special gifts for her friends. One such case was number "22," an untitled canvas of a miniature basket baby. She presented the jewel-like painting as a wedding gift to Mrs. Lena Howell Faulkner, a former art pupil, on June 28, 1894. As was often the case, a short poem written by Grace accompanied the painting to its new home:

How do you do
   I've come to stay awhile
For deep-down in my heart is hid
   A fond desire to be your kid
I'll never naughty be or bawl
   Unless you turn me to the wall

Returning to a larger canvas, Grace next painted *To-Tole, The Star*. While not of the same magnitude as *Yokia Treasures*, the portrait of a young Indian girl in an elaborate feather headdress and buckskin cloak was a major work. It has found its way into the collection of the Oakland Museum. The headdress was, even in 1894, a relatively recent addition to Pomo garments, used in the Ghost Dance religious ceremony. Rather large, it consisted of many long, slender withes, each tipped with several feathers.

In use, the decoration was fastened to the scalp by wooden hairpins through its skullcap and framework. Each withe projected at right angles from the foundation, to produce a hemispherical headdress sometimes as much as a yard in diameter.

To have captured with such detail every nuance of the garments, without consideration of the exquisite facial features found in *To-Tole*, would have done justice to any painter in any era.

By autumn of the year, the public's interest in the young woman artist had once again increased. Demand grew, not only to know more about Grace Hudson and her work, but also to find what she looked like. The *Illustrated Pacific States*, in its September, 1894 issue, published an article containing a formal portrait of Grace and the following account:

Baby Bunting
Private Collection

We give in this number a portrait of the widely-known artist, Mrs. Grace Carpenter Hudson, which surely cannot fail to please. The handsome face which smiles back at us from the page would be most attractive, even if the interest arising from her fame as an artist should not lend its added charm.

There is an indication of her genius in the bright, magnetic expression, which all will notice, and, besides, there is such a suggestion of sweetness and pleasantry in her face that none can discredit the loveable character they evidence.

Mrs. Hudson enjoys a wide and well-deserved reputation for her pictures of Indians. She has shown remarkable skill in depicting the dark-skinned children of the wigwam and the forest, and gives us glimpses of wild babyhood, as rare as they are touching. In her unique specialty, she stands without rival. Her pictures are lifelike, and her work is the more worthy of commendation in consideration of the difficulties to be surmounted in painting from such peculiar and busy, unpathetic models.

Born amid rural scenes in Mendocino County, of parents who are as honest and truthful as God's harmonious nature surrounding her birthplace, Mrs. Hudson enjoys a combination of advantages rarely enjoyed by any other natural-born artist.

Mr. Morris, of Morris and Kennedy, who is acknowledged to be an excellent critic, says of her work, "We have had for sale and on exhibition a number of Mrs. Hudson's pictures, and they have universally received the highest admiration and praise. Some of her larger canvases bring as high as $500, and smaller ones from $150 up. Such prices give ample testimony of her skill and popularity. I know of no California artist who gives promise of greater success than lies in power to achieve; and I believe, with time and a wider field, her talent will acquire national fame."

. . . Personally, Mrs. Hudson is bright and charming, as her portrait suggests. Of the brunette type, slight and graceful, she is gifted with uncommon attractions; but, besides, one finds in her that power of intellect and brilliance of perception which in themselves seem winning charms enough.

The article included an illustration of her seventh canvas of 1894, *Baby Bunting*, number "24." It was another large canvas, with dimensions of 31- by 30-inches, and was exhibited at the California State Fair later in the year. For its subject matter, Grace returned to the basket babies of the Pomo that were, by now, familiar in every detail. Both the child, and the usually watchful mixed-breed dog at its side, were depicted sleeping.

For the first time, Grace explored the prospect of grouping several of her paintings. For subjects, she chose three young children approximately five years of age. To have captured a fleeting deer, a dove on the wing, or a butterfly would have been an easier task. Numbering the studies "25"-"27," all three could be considered miniatures but, together, form a work of a stature that was comparable to her larger canvases.

Three other paintings were completed in 1894. Two of these, *Who Comes?*, and *Mamma*, numbers "28" and "29" respectively, brought additional accolades to Grace Hudson.

Who Comes?, or *Cho-ba wa-dee*, was another lifesized portrait of a Pomo baby, with dimensions of 30- by 30-inches. It was exhibited for a time at Morris and Kennedy's galleries in San Francisco, then at Thurber's in Chicago, but it was at the Denver Art Club show in April, 1896 that it received the recognition it justly deserved. *The Denver Post*, April 20, 1896, commented:

The first picture towards which all eyes turn among the oils is the Cho-be Wa-dee? *(Who comes?) of Grace Hudson of Ukiah, California. The subject of this most charming sketch is an Indian baby, just old enough to look knowing. The papoose is thong-bound in a little willow cradle in a semi-upright position. The sides of the cradle shut out from view the approach of someone or something, judging from the alert and half-frightened expression of the dusky little tot.*

The picture is exquisite in its conception and detail and withal so natural, even to those who have never seen an Indian baby, that nothing is left to the imagination of the observer, so forcefully are the thoughts and surroundings of the infant transmitted to canvas. One expects almost momentarily a view of the intruder and, with it, to hear a startled cry from the little occupant of the little cradle.

This is as fine a piece of work from an amateur, or any other, as has ever been seen by the Artist's Club in Denver.

About a year after the portrait was sold to Miers Fisher of Denver, a photograph reproduced from Grace's file photograph taken by her father appeared in *Frank Leslie's Popular Monthly*, mistitled *Hard Times*. This was likely another example of admirers renaming a painting, but could have been the result of a printing error. Mr. Fisher, at any rate, was sufficiently interested to write to the artist in Ukiah:

Dear Madam:
I am the highly satisfied owner of one of your masterpieces, which I purchased through Mr. Newcomb of this city, and I desire to know more about it from yourself. It was sold to me under the name of Who Comes? *and under that name I placed it on exhibition, with a few explanatory remarks on a card to satisfy its admirers, who were keeping one person busy answering questions. As the name seemed appropriate to me, I, of course, gave what I thought to be its meaning in these words. "A crying papoose, with a dirt-besmeared face, left temporarily by its mother, arrests its tears for a moment and looks expectantly and hopefully around, attracted by the sound of approaching footsteps." It is a type of what has been seen daily on every corner of the streets of Denver 35 years ago, but what will never be seen there again. Last evening I found in* Frank Leslie's Popular Monthly *my picture reproduced as an illustration in an article by Ninetta Eames, in which it was called* Hard Times.
. . .My picture is either the copy of an original with another name, or my picture has been copied.

Mr. Fisher went on to explain further his doubts and anxiety regarding the

Who Comes?
Location Unknown

36

stature of his painting. Grace undoubtedly relieved his apprehension by return mail, explaining her custom of photographing each painting before it left her studio in Ukiah.

In the intervening years since Grant had left for Michigan to continue his education and the first years of Grace's marriage to Dr. Hudson, Grant had returned to the West Coast. Foregoing a career in law, he had joined instead the ranks of the journalists, much to Reel's delight. A short time later, he was elected President of the San Francisco Press Club.

Perhaps it was with this in mind that Grace completed *Mamma*, number "29." On November 21, 1894, Grace received correspondence from the Press Club:

Your letter to the President of the Press Club, containing a splendid offer of one of your pictures for our new rooms, was read at the meeting of the board of managers yesterday and referred to me as chairman of the library and art committee. I am directed by the board to thank you most sincerely and assure you that your kindness to the homeless men of the pen is most gratefully appreciated. It is needless for me to add that a picture done by one so well known as yourself in art circles will be most acceptable to the Press Club.

On January 13 of the following year, a second letter from the Press Club librarian was received by Grace:

I am directed by the board of managers of the San Francisco Press Club to thank you, in the name of the entire club membership, for the beautiful painting that you so generously sent us on the eve of our occupancy of our new home. Among the treasures of that home, Mamma *is the dearest for many reasons. First, because you were the first to send us a genuine work of art; second, that it is the first beautiful painting to be placed upon our walls; and third, because it came from Mrs. Grace Hudson, who [sic] we all admire for her exquisite work and thoughtful generosity.*

To say that your picture is admired by all our members but mildly conveys the expressions heard on all sides. We take particular pleasure in calling attention of visitors to Mamma *the first picture presented to the club.*

Please accept this poor expression of the gratitude of the Press Club as coming from the entire membership.

Four years later, on May 17, 1899, Grace received from W. C. Brunner, secretary of the club, a letter which conferred upon her an honor which she regarded as a rather special tribute:

I am pleased to inform you that, at the last meeting of the board of managers of the Press Club, you were elected an honorary member of the club.

We are anxious in some way to show our appreciation for the kindness you had shown us long ago. Let me assure you that we consider your present of Mamma Indian baby *one of the most valued of our art treasures, which might have been acknowledged in this manner long ago, were it not for the fact that we wished to pass this resolution without the knowledge of your brother, and our president, Mr. Grant Carpenter. Luckily we caught him absent from the meeting yesterday, which gave us the desired opportunity.*

In the name of the Press Club, let me thank you again.

Unfortunately, these letters had an unhappy postscript. After hanging at the Press Club for nearly a decade, *Mamma* burned in the fire following the 1906 earthquake, together with *The First Pang*, canvas number "41," which she donated to the club a few years later.

Only one remaining canvas was completed during 1894. Titled *Early Birds* and numbered "30," Grace chose as her subject a woodpecker and a little boy, evidently just awakened from slumber. The bird is as surprised that someone is at home as is the unclothed host at having a caller. The pose of disgust might indicate that the two had met before under similar circumstances, and the little host is agitated at the recurrence of the disturbance of his early-morning nap.

Without question, by the end of 1894 Grace Hudson enjoyed a popularity that extended across the entire nation. She and her husband now shared a common interest—the culture, people and artifacts of the Pomo Indians—as well as an endearing love for one another. Through the medium of magazines, newspapers, and exhibition in far-away galleries and expositions, they had made Ukiah and the northern valley of California an enduring part of the world of western art.

CHAPTER 4

THE CENTURY'S END

Growth and Recognition in the World of Art

I F THE YEARS between the completion of Grace Hudson's first numbered work, *National Thorn*, and her last painting for the year 1894 were ones filled with national recognition of her talent and growing maturity, those spanning the last of the century could be described best as a period of bounty.

During the half-decade from 1895-1900, Grace completed 125 major canvases, adding to the rapidly expanding notebook of her finished oils. Quality did not suffer from her increased production, but the dimension of many of the new works were were reduced. More than half were 80 square inches or less. Equally evident, however, was an increased mastery of style, expanded subject matter that continued her thematic statement about the Pomo Indians.

Except for three portraits, the Indian children remained her sole subject. Grace captured their moods, expressions, thoughts, actions, dispositions, and humor. Increasingly, she concentrated on refining her observations of a small segment of the West. In doing so, she expanded her vision and made the Indian people uniquely her own.

Grace Hudson had been a child raised among the Native Americans, and she understood them better than many of her contemporaries. Unlike many other artists who journeyed west in search of a proud and noble race, Grace was comfortable with the day-to-day life of men and women whom she knew best as her friends and acquaintances.

A Sunday issue of the *San Francisco Call* for October 27, 1895 attempted to answer the question of how Grace Hudson had been able to produce, time after time, such remarkable paintings of Indian children:

Mrs. Grace Hudson, the young California artist who has made herself famous by painting papooses, wiped her brushes and dropped into a chair in the ivy-covered veranda of her studio at Ukiah. "Now I'll tell you all you want to know and more, too, perhaps. I have much to contend against, but, with the exercise of a little ingenuity and a great deal of perseverance, I am able to catch an Indian baby in some interesting attitude or position. There's the little fellow lying on his back, trying to get his brown little foot in his mouth," said the lady, pointing to one of her pictures. "That baby looks as if he never did anything but laugh, but I had to feed him gumdrops to get the little rascal to look pleasant. That gave me the expression. The pose and coloring had to be done without the model.

"When I see a baby that I want to paint, I cannot borrow it for an indefinite period by telling its parents it's the sweetest thing on earth. I have to kidnap it first

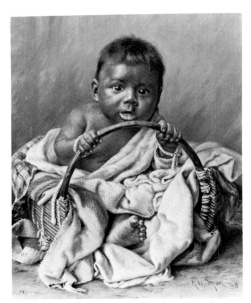

Jimmie (Gallery Title)
Private Collection

and then overcome the natural inclination of a baby to do everything except what is desired.

"There is a popular superstition among the Indians that neither arguments nor bribes will shake. To be sketched or photographed is sure to bring some terrible calamity down on the head of the subject. If it is not a speedy death, it is disfigurement for life, or, at the very least, blindness. As most Pomo Indians become blind in their old age from sitting all their lives over the smoke of their campfires, their superstition never lacks confirmation. Why, if these Indians here in Ukiah knew I painted their babies, I would be regarded as a murderess in a chamber of horrors. When I want a subject, I first have to find a squaw with a papoose. If the child's face suits me, I enter into negotiations with the mother to do some work for me, usually scrubbing floors or cleaning windows. She leaves the baby strapped up in his basket and braced up against the side of the house, where it will be under her eye. The next maneuver is to get possession of that papoose. I must make it cry so that I may have some reasonable excuse for taking an interest in it. There is where Mascot, our St. Bernard, 'does his turn,' as the theatrical people say. Here, Mascot, speak.

"An orange and white St. Bernard, almost as big as a Shetland pony, bounced up out of the cool ivy and let out a roar that fairly shook the house.

"That will usually make an Indian baby cry," explained Mrs. Hudson. "If it doesn't frighten the baby, it does the mother, and I have to go to the rescue in any event. Mascot just loves to poke his cold nose into a baby's face when it is strapped up hand and foot and perfectly helpless. So the mother is glad enough to let me take the papoose inside, where it will be safe. I promise to take good care of it and to buy it a new dress and to give it some beads. In a jiffy, I have that baby propped up in the light against the front door of my studio. Then comes the task of getting a sketch of one fleeting expression on the face of the baby, indicative of interest in life. They are regular little stoics. They will sit and stare without blinking an eye or moving a muscle, while I perform the most grotesque antics in order to provoke a laugh. I can occasionally interest them by giving them something to eat, but there is always something about the way they accept food from me that reminds me of the caged animal. I worked three days on a baby before I could get a smile, and only then by putting on a feathered headdress and dancing around like an Apache medicine man. I worried, tormented, bullied and frightened the one poor little fellow for two days, trying to make him cry. I grew ashamed of myself and gave it up.

"But to have them sleep is another thing. I have almost been tempted to chloroform them. It seems to me that they never sleep. I have rocked them and sung to them till I was hoarse and dizzy, and still their big brown eyes that looked like painted porcelain would stare at me just as unblinkingly as if there was no such thing as sleep.

"Have any of the babies you painted died?" was asked.

"Yes, one. It was my namesake. Its mother promised to name it after me, but it turned out to be a boy. Had it been a girl, its name would have been Grace Hudson Billy-Bow-legs (the family name is quite up-to-date, being hyphenated). The poor baby struggled along under the name of Mr. Dr. Hudson Billy-Bow-Legs for a little over a year before he died. If its mother ever knew that I had painted him, she would have held me responsible for his death."

Another interesting interview for the *San Francisco Examiner*, April 21, 1895 answered the question: "Why do you stay here?"

"Well, there are less distractions in Ukiah than there would be in San Francisco,

40

and, besides, I am near my subjects. I am having a time with my last baby," turning to light an easel on which was an unfinished painting of an infant. "The mother is Old Mary, our washwoman, but it would never do to let her know now why I carry off the baby while she is working. Indians have a superstition that death may occur from having their image reproduced. Since I commenced this, Mary has been ill; so I have to paint from two other babies, which I manage to smuggle into the studio at different times. I am seldom able to get the same child all through the painting of a picture, for an Indian can seldom be relied upon for anything and rarely comes when he agrees to, unless he is hungry."

The wardrobe, kept by the Indian painter for purposes of art, is not the least novel feature of the Hudson studio. The walls are ornamented with strings of Indian money and beads, bows, arrows, spears, whistles, war clubs, a fantastic dance dress and headgear, the curious paraphernalia of the mysterious "medicine man," a chief's blanket of squirrel skins and, in the storeroom off the hop-trellised porch, a motley assortment of picturesque rags, with which the artist decorates her sitters.

Untitled
Private Collection

Clearly, the influence of Dr. Hudson's interest in the ethnology and anthropology of the Pomo was beginning to be seen in Graces's art. Besides the collection of basketry, articles of ceremonial clothing, and other artifacts, Grace had expanded her knowledge of the Indian families themselves.

In time, her understanding of the Pomo prompted her to attempt multiple canvases of related subject matter. One of the adult portraits which Grace Hudson produced in 1895, number "40," was of an Indian girl named Mollie and was titled *Powley's Sweetheart*. Grace was well acquainted with Mollie, and her familiarity with her subject was evident in the painting. Ninetta Eames wrote in *Frank Leslie's Popular Monthly* for April, 1897:

Powley's Sweetheart is one of the most pleasing of Grace Hudson's paintings. There is a look of actual presence about it that is consumately good. The flesh is indescribably realistic. That soft blending of rose and purple which is characteristic of Indian skin during the summer, when frequent river bathing is the favorite pastime. The original of the picture is a comely maiden of 'Pinoleville,' the local name for the Ukiah rancheria. She wears her hair cut short, which is the custom of her people when mourning for some dead relative. But in this instance, the blue-black locks were voluntarily sacrificed to get money to buy oranges to send a disreputable father, who was in prison. The family disgrace seems not to weigh upon the spirits of the daughter, for a word or look sets the dimples to playing around her red, red mouth.

Powley's Sweetheart
Location Unknown

A portrait of the young man of Mollie's affection soon followed. Again, her subject was well known by the artist. Evidently, however, Powley's romance with Mollie was a youthful infatuation, for another woman, Joseppa, became his wife.

As usual, Grace Hudson's skill with brush and oil was sufficient to arouse comment. When the paintings of Mollie and Powley were placed on exhibition in an art room in San Francisco, three onlookers were overheard to relate the following series of comments:

"Well, *she* paints Indians!" said the first.

. The companion next to him replied, excitedly, "She *paints* Indians!" Whereupon the third and final play upon emphasis was made as the last gentleman declared, with conviction, "She paints *Indians*!"

Nor did Grace Hudson's interest in her subjects end with the completion of a portrait. Powley was later selected by her husband to attend the Mid-Winter Fair in San Francisco. A great deal of persuasion and diffident assurance of a safe return was necessary before the Indian could be convinced to travel so far from home. Many of the Pomo had never forgotten the theft of their children a few years earlier by untruthful whites, who sold the youngsters into slavery. Upon assurance of food, a small salary, free access to concessions, and the privilege of selling their crafts, Powley joined the small number of Indians that had consented to attend.

Powley was accompanied by his wife and his six month old stepson, Billy. The little band took bows and arrows, and the women wove intricate and beautiful baskets for the passersby.

The Pomo who attended the festival proved a great attraction at the Fair. When they arrived home with so many wonderful tales of San Francisco they became the envy of the entire tribe, and Powley assumed an importance beyond his dreams. The name Powley seemed inadequate to his new stature, and of his own volition he became known as Jeff Dick.

Grace Hudson attempted not only to record a vanishing race on canvas; she very frequently included items of their culture which held anthropological significance. Her painting number "34," *The Little Piper*, provides one such example. The young Pomo in this canvas plays a typical four-holed flute of the tribe. At each of the holes in these elderberry-wood flutes, a square area was flattened. The fingertips were fitted into the flattened areas while playing the instrument, modifying the sound produced as the breath passed into the trimmed end. In use the instrument was normally played by men, chiefly as a pastime, but occasionally was referred to as a "lover's flute."

Other examples of Grace Hudson's attention to detail in choosing subject matter for her paintings may be found throughout the entire series of her work. One of the larger canvases of 1895, number "45" was called *Mendocino Products*. It concentrated for its subject on two of the most important aspects of Indian life, a child and his faithful dog. In the canvas, a child sleeps after a long morning spent helping with the hop harvest. Coolness in the shade of the vines and softness of the deerskin, coupled with a sense of security afforded by the watchful eyes of his faithful companion, convey a delightful sense of tranquility.

Mendocino Products
Location Unknown

Little dogs such as the one seen in *Mendocino Products* had made their appearance in her first canvas, *National Thorn*, painted in 1891 and was truly representative of the life of the Pomo; rarely was an Indian family seen without a dog. Grace was so pleased with the result of the dog-child subject that she made many similar portraits, though few approached *Mendocino Products* in size. The painting was exhibited successfully at the California State Fair, where it received a cash prize in the Art Department.

Few events of everyday life escaped Grace Hudson's attention. An upset stomach caused by eating too many green apples, as in *The First Pang*, number "41," or a minor injury such as is found in *Andy with a Cut Finger*, number "49," prompted her to as careful and serious studies as might be found for subjects dealing with the most intricate ceremony or colorful legend.

Without question, by the end of 1895, Grace Hudson had achieved commendation throughout the entire scope of the art world. Her reputation had become national, even international. Articles on her had appeared in newspapers in New York, Chicago, Denver, and, of course, San Francisco. She had been recognized with awards at the Mechanics Fair in San Francisco and the State Fair in Sacramento. One canvas, *Blue Monday*, number "66," was accepted in 1896 for the first Carnegie competition in Pittsburgh bringing Grace together with a distinguished company that included George de Forest Brush, William M. Chase, F. S. Church, Kenyon Cox, Bruce Crane, Frederick Deilman, Alexander Hansen, Winslow Homer, Walter Shirlaw, Abbott H. Thayer, Elihu Vedden, E. L. Weeks, Irving R. Wiles, and Whistler.

Blue Monday
Location Unknown

The list of her collectors included such names as Brannon, Morrell and Shattuck from Boston; Hamilton, Johnson, Hirsch, Masticks, Van Sicklin, Wheeler, Warfield, Kowalsky, Nathan, Guggenheim, Pond and Phelan from the San Francisco bay area; Fisher and McCutchen from Denver; and Wheat and Huntington from Los Angeles. It was veritable who's who of art collectors.

The picture-loving public found genuine beauty in her images of native Californians from Mendocino County and recognized in Grace Hudson a talent of stature. The art world referred to her with admiration as a "pot boiler," their term for a painter whose canvases sold as rapidly as they were finished. Indeed, her commercial success and its accompanying demand must have played an increasing role in the number of canvases which she produced.

Grace Carpenter
Private Collection

In 1896 alone, she prepared 24 canvases; all were sold upon completion. In 1897, 30 more Hudsons left the growing studio in Ukiah; they too, quickly found homes among the world's great collections. Without doubt, Grace Hudson had passed beyond the realm of ordinary success.

Even so, the artist must have felt a need to withdraw from the images that had made her so successful. On few occasions in her entire career did she paint subjects other than Indians: number "56," was a portrait of her sister, May Carpenter Ellis, seated in a wicker rocker. After completion of the painting, it was shipped to May. According to the family, as the package was unwrapped, one of the Ellis children commented loudly that the painting looked exactly like her mother, adding a naive critic's view to that of the more jaded press. To this day, the painting remains part of the Ellis family collection.

In 1897 she again paused from more familiar subject matter. This time, she prepared a portrait of one of her nieces, Grace Carpenter, number "92." When compared to her usual subject matter, the painting was a study in opposites—from ragged shirts and dirty blankets to green lawn and daintly lace; from a buckskin blouse to puff sleeves; from bow and arrow to violin. Like the portrait of May, Grace's namesake was proud of her portrait, and it remained a cherished family possession.

Two paintings from this period were studies of Pomo male ceremonial costumes. The daily attire of the tribe was meager, but on the occasion of ceremonies their dress could be elaborate. There were several intricate Pomo ceremonies, each with its own special costume and body painting. During warmer weather, dances were held out-of-doors; on other occasions of secrecy or inclement weather, partially buried dance houses were used.

Perhaps the most striking of all the Hudson paintings of ceremonies is *The Seed Conjurer* number "61," which features many unique and unusual articles of dance dress. The most important item of the apparel shown is the feathered mantles, which form a shirt-like covering. These mantles were usually fashioned from the plumage of the buzzard, or turkey vulture, fastened to a foundation of net, then layered to create an appearance of fullness and splendor. The garment was usually tied under the arms so as to cover the wearer's back and lower body. In *The Dancer*, number "136," the mantle may be seen.

Various head ornaments are depicted in a number of Hudson paintings. The Pomo feather headdress usually consisted of a cap, made from hawk or crow feathers of small size, drawn together so that they formed an immense topknot which fell in all directions. This cap was fastened to the head with long wooden skewers similar to hat pins. The flicker, or yellow-hammer, quillband was more common. These bands were worn horizontally across the forehead, by both men and women. They usually did not exceed two feet in length, with the middle six or eight inches bound tightly to the forehead by strings which wound around the head to tie behind. The rest of the band extended to both sides of the head, floating freely in the air as the dancer moved.

The Seed Conjurer
Private Collection

Only long feathers, from the wings and tail of the flicker, were used in making the bands, and they frequently required the plumage of more than 30 birds to fill a complete headdress.

To construct the headdress, the quills were pierced with an awl, then strung on very fine cords. Because the shafts of the larger feathers were bright reddish or golden colored, while the tips were a rich black, most were stripped down to the colored quill. Only a few were left untrimmed, and a delicate border of black-tipped feathers formed the dark edge of the band. Occasionally, the headdress was ornamented by adding shell beads, pendants, or quail plumes.

When Grace Hudson found willing suitable subjects, it was not uncommon for her to paint them several times. Some multiple portraits were made over a period of time and depicted the subject at various ages; other studies painted the same person several times in the course of a year. One example is the boy seen in *Greenie*, number "62." He was painted four times during 1896, resulting in canvases numbered "70," "73," and "77," besides the work previously mentioned.

Another of Grace Hudson's favorite models was Rosa Peters, who first made her debut in Hudson's paintings in 1895, the subject of *Rosie*, a medium-sized canvas, number "36." Rosa and Grace became good friends. As a result, more than 30 canvases were completed of her and her family—Moose, Mary Angel, Rosita, and William—over a span of time that lasted for 20 years.

Despite Grace's multiple use of a single subject, it is frequently difficult to determine the sex of children in many of her paintings. Had she not recorded Greenie's name along with other data about his finished portraits, one might assume the rosy-cheeked youngster was a girl. His nightshirt-styled garment was probably sewn by Grace herself.

As Grace Hudson continued to explore her medium and subjects, she was also receiving recognition as a leading illustrator. An article appeared in the February 19, 1896 issue of the New York *Journal* describing her success:

In Mendocino County, one of the most northern as well as most picturesque counties of California, is to be found the quaint little studio of the well-known Indian painter, Grace Hudson. Mrs. Hudson is a fine type of the Western girl, who, feeling in herself the desire to paint, and having no means to reach those art centers where people may be taught to paint, determined to paint just the same. With the exception of a short period in a San Francisco art school, she is self-taught. One is tempted to say, "a self-made woman." And today in all the leading art journals she is known as "one of the greatest American Indian painters."

She has surmounted what to a woman of less persistent perseverance would have seemed crushing and overpowering obstacles. Her lot having been cast in one of the most picturesque but wildest and most isolated parts of California, she turned her attention to the subjects nearest at hand. Her greatest interest has always been to catch the varying expressions of the human face. She was not long in deciding to make the faithful portrayal of the Indian her life study.

Her home has always been the original home of the Pomo tribe and she has ample opportunity to watch their every habit and custom. The child life interested her the most and through these she has reached her greatest success, although her pictures of Captain John and other old patriarchs of the tribe are considered especially valuable as characteristic types of a race that is fast dying out. Most of her models are, she laughingly says, "stolen." The task seems a difficult one indeed.

The article was accompanied by an engraved illustration of Grace Hudson surrounded by four of her paintings.

The February 28, 1896 issue of the Ukiah *Dispatch-Democrat* also described her magazine illustration;

One of the leading articles in the Cosmopolitan Magazine *for March is entitled "Upland Pastures," by Ninetta Eames with illustrations from original drawings by Grace Hudson, the well-known artist of this place. The article describes sheep raising in California and the material for it was secured on Doc Standley's ranch at Sherwood. The article opens with a half-page illustration entitled "Doc Standley." It represents Doc sitting on his hunting mule with his hounds standing about. The article shows careful preparation by the writer and is exceedingly well written, despite the fact that the writer throws a little too much dialect into Standley's conversation.*

As the Cosmopolitan, *with its circulation of half-million copies a month, is the greatest magazine in the world, "Upland Pastures" will give Mendocino County and one of its leading industries considerable advertising and some of our local people much celebrity. Especially will Mrs. Hudson's host of admirers be pleased to see that her talent as an artist is fast carrying her to the front rank among the leading illustrators of America.*

Coincidentally, the article marked one of the last magazine stories to be illustrated by Grace. She increasingly turned her attention to her numbered oils, and Grace Hudson drawings no longer appeared in such periodicals after 1897.

The quest of the public for more information about Grace Hudson and her life in the rugged northern California mountains prompted Ninetta Eames to write once again about the petite artist, this time describing her hunting activities. The piece, entitled, "A Mendocino Diana Shooting Turtle Doves in Russian River Groves," appeared in the September 6, 1896, *San Francisco Chronicle:*

Painting Indian babies and dusky Madonnas is not the only thing Grace Hudson is doing these hot summer days, though picture lovers might judge so from the number of her works recently exhibited and sold in San Francisco, New York, and Boston. A call at the Hudson studio in Ukiah late one afternoon found the artist just coming forth, jauntily dressed in short corduroy skirt, a brown alpaca shooting jacket over a blue shirt blouse, her pretty head surmounted by a soft felt hat with a rakish tassel on the side. She was carrying a light twelve-gauge gun. By her side strode an enormous white and orange coated St. Bernard. The two made a charming picture.

Grace was described as a crack shot.

After a dove hunt there is no vestige of artistic proportion left to the artist's lovely figure. The inside pouches of her shooting jacket are so stuffed with game that they bulge like panniers on the hips, and the effect is most grotesque, but all this she enjoys as zestfully as the rest of the hunting experience.

Grace Hudson's interest in birds did not end with those that fell prey to her shotgun. In her paintings, they continued to provide striking counterpoint to her carefully composed human subjects. One, *The Quail Hunter*, number "69," illustrated an important male role.

The painting introduced Thomas Mitchell to the Hudson gallery. Like many of her other subjects, a lifetime friendship developed between the artist and the Mitchells. Tom, his wives, his children, and even his grandchildren became the subjects for more than 100 other Hudson paintings, easily the most numerous represen-

Quail Hunter
Private Collection

tation of any Indian family. Several of Tom Mitchell's children were painted as many as 20 times, from earliest infancy to adulthood.

Perhaps no other species of bird was more esteemed for food than the colorful valley quail. The small birds were usually taken with basketry quail traps or quail nets, while the mountain quail, a slightly larger bird, was shot with bow and arrows. A light bow was used, together with an arrow constructed of elderberry wood and greasewood, or mountain mahogany. A carefully worked obsidian point was bound to the shaft by tight wrappings of sinew or other binding.

For such a weapon, the tiny quail were an illusive and difficult target, one that required great skill and much patience. When successful, the catch was prepared by the women. Each bird was cooked directly on the hot coals of an open fire. Feathers were singed off, and the meat was broiled.

The Quail Hunter that survives seems to be a re-creation by the artist, for the original canvas was an oval composition that was damaged by falling glass at the Schussler Brothers Gallery during the San Francisco earthquake and fire. In its original form, the painting was reproduced as a cover illustration for *Western Field* magazine in its October, 1903 edition.

Many of the Hudson paintings traveled widely before purchase, but few journeyed more than a portrait titled, appropriately, *The Runaway*, number "72." A striking composition of two Indian youngsters, it was exhibited at the Tennessee Exposition in 1897, the Denver Exposition in 1898, the Cincinnati Museum Association in 1898, and again in Chicago, in 1899. Its whereabouts today is unknown to all but its owners.

Grace Hudson's style of eliciting response from a viewer is well illustrated in *The Runaway*. In the painting, Annie Mitchell assumed the duties often demanded of an older sister. Whatever mischief that the little one must have been pursuing when rescued by her sister evidently was of such an enjoyable sort as to provoke the strong disapproval evident in the canvas. Besides arousing curiosity as to the events, the painting illustrated Grace's superb ability to capture a fleeting moment in time. Such a pose would have been tiring and uncomfortable, even for subjects with more patience.

Ironically, *The Runaway* also caused a bitter misunderstanding to erupt between Grace and her twin brother, Grant. In February, 1897, Grant, then employed by the *San Francisco Evening Post*, penned a supposed interview with his sister, Grace Hudson.

Baby Fitch
Location Unknown

The Indian paintings of Mrs. Grace Hudson, which of late have attracted so much attention from artists and lovers of art, have arroused an interest in the public generally, this about equally divided between the talented artist herself and quaint subjects she so faithfully portrays.

Who is Mrs. Hudson? Where does she get her Indian models? How does she ever get them to pose for her? These are the questions that are asked almost daily, and some of the absurd answers that are given—based more on ignorance than envy—have done the unassuming little woman gross injustice.

Mrs. Hudson has been described as an ignorant little country girl, with some artistic talent developed (slightly) by the assiduous use of chalk on a board fence, who ultimately married an Indian and learned to color photographs of the half-caste issue of that marriage—whereat Mrs. Hudson only smiles and continues unperturbed in the work that pleases admirers of true art. Of herself, the artist ever has little to say, but she is enthusiastic in everything that pertains to her work, and her studio is always open to all who feel interested enough to pay it a visit.

Mrs. Hudson was once a little country girl. She enjoys the distinction of having selected a log cabin for her birthplace, thereby qualifying herself for the presiden-

cy of the United States. She was born in Potter Valley, one of the garden spots of Mendocino, about sixteen miles northeast of Ukiah. While attending the public schools at Ukiah, she manifested some artistic talent, and, after laying the foundation of her education, took up art in connection with her other studies. She entered the San Francisco Art School in 1880 and, under the guidance of that able old instructor, Virgil Williams, progressed so rapidly that in 1882 she was awarded the Alvord Medal, after competing with many students who have since made their marks in the profession. Joullin, the well-known artist, was one of the unsuccessful competitors. Afterwards, Mrs. Hudson studied landscape work under Tojetti, the elder. Since then she has pursued her work with a perserverance that made success inevitable and placed her in the front rank of the world's artists. Several years ago she became the wife of Dr. J. W. Hudson, a Southerner, who is at present practicing his profession in Ukiah, where Mrs. Hudson has her studio.

Cornered
Location Unknown

The early life of the artist was spent among the Indians of Mendocino, and it was but natural that their picturesque character should attract the attention of an artist who has shown such marked originality in her work. A field of art that had never been invaded by pencil or brush was opened to her, and she was quick to take advantage of delights it contained. There is where she procured her subjects and where she continues to find them, though the advances of civilization are rapidly depopulating the "rancherios" and destroying the distinguishing characteristics of the aboriginal race. Dr. Hudson is an enthusiastic ethnologist, and his collection of Indian baskets and curios, as Mrs. Hudson's paintings, have already secured to science facts concerning the rapidly vanishing people that are of inestimable value. How Indians are secured as models are best told by the artist herself.

"That has been my greatest obstacle," said she. "Superstition is part of an Indian's nature, and it is so firmly rooted that neither reason nor experience can shake it. Anything that their simple natures cannot comprehend at a glance is be-believed to be the work of the evil spirit. I can remember when no Indian in Mendocino County would touch a written message, but would carry a letter in the end of a split stick at arm's length and poke it frantically at the first white he met. Some few learned to read and write at the reservation schools, and, now that the mysteries of chirography have been explained to their satisfaction, they no longer stand in awe of it.

"The telephone and telegraph are utterly beyond the comprehension of even the most civilized, and no bribe would tempt one to tamper with either. Photography, however, is to them even more wonderful, for they see tangible results produced from intangiblity. They regard the photograph as part of the personality of the subject secured by machinations of the evil spirit, and nothing will induce one of them to part with what he firmly believes is a part of his face. Some few of them, however, will sit to be sketched, for they can readily understand that process.

"One of my models was a very old Indian, who accepted the opportunity to earn a few dollars only after years of deprivation and disease and with starvation staring him in the face. He firmly expected to die under the ordeal, but, with the remark that he couldn't live long anyway, took his seat like a stoic and maintained his pose without so much as the twitching of a muscle for hours at a time. When I had finished with him and demonstrated that the occupation was not necessarily fatal, I tried to induce him to bring his grandchildren to sit for me; but no bribe that I could offer him would influence him to risk it. I have also secured as models some young men and women, but the superstitious fear of the camera clings to it all. The impossibility of the practice which has been imputed to me—that of posing and photographing my models and then painting them over a solar print—is, therefore apparent. One who can do that will accomplish

47

much more than I have ever succeeded in doing. He will break down the impregnable barrier to the thorough civilization of the Indian—superstition.

"The painting of Indian babies, however, is another matter. They cannot pose even if their parents would permit. The only aid I get in my work is a tiny snapshot photograph. When I want a subject, I employ the mother of the child to do some work, and, while she is occupied, resort to all sorts of artifices to get a photograph of the child. My calling is well known among the Indians, and so they guard their children with a most vigilant eye when I am near; but I usually succeed in outwitting them. One day I will get a photograph of a baby's face and the next day a hand or a foot. Sometimes I get a little boy of the neighborhood to pose for me until I can sketch the outline and then I put the little Indian face on him. Nearly all of my pictures are what might be termed composites. The Runaway, now on exhibition in San Francisco, illustrates my method as well as any. I employed a squaw with a petulent baby two years of age to do some work. While she was busy, I sent my little niece out to entice the crying child away. She gave it some candy and induced it to accompany her. When they got opposite my place of concealment and out of sight of the mother, my niece seized the child under the arms from behind, held it and gave it a shake. As it commenced to wiggle and cry, I photographed it, and just had time to hide again before the anxious mother came running to see what had happened. The baby's pose I caught very nicely; but I had to put a little Indian girl on the canvas in place of my golden-haired niece.

"Of course, in the coloring of flesh tints, I have no aid except the brief glimpses the anxious mothers will give me of their babies. My labor would be immeasureably lightened if I could paint directly from living models instead of a small photograph, too often blurred by a bad light or improper focus."

The March 6, 1897 issue of *Town Talk*, a rival publication, included an entire column of Grace Hudson's scathing response to Grant's suggestion that she worked from photographs, not life:

L. G. Carpenter, editor of the "Out of the Groove" column of the Post, does not supply the readers of that journal with all the good stories that he knows. The story about the "write-up" that he gave his sister, Grace Hudson, the talented artist, whose fame as a painter of studies from Indian life has extended all over the country, is kept by him for private circulation. It was at the request of Hugh Hume, proprietor of the Post, that Carpenter wrote a special article on the subject of his sister's paintings, and the difficulty that she experiences in obtaining Indian sketches. He explained that a superstition prevails among the Indians that causes them to be filled with dread whenever they find that they have been photographed or sketched, and that, owing to their reluctance to pose, the artist is compelled to resort to all sorts of ruses or operate her Kodak without their knowledge. But the fact is that Grace Hudson does not depend on a Kodak for her studies. She is a thorough artist, and the imputation that she uses a Kodak to assist her art is not to her liking. Yet Carpenter, whose knowledge of the technique of his sister's profession is somewhat limited, labored under the delusion that she would be highly pleased with the special article, until he received a letter from her suggesting that he should confine his journalistic work to "Out of the Groove" topics, and informing him that her worst enemy could not have done her a greater injustice than to represent that the phases of Indian Life depicted by her upon canvas were mere copies of photographs. In reply to this letter, he informed her that there were seven different kinds of fools in the world and that he believed himself to be a resplendent combination of the group.

Only Grant's prompt apology prevented the incident from becoming a distressing family rift.

On January 8, 1897, the women of the Century Club of San Francisco held a reception of Grace Hudson. Indian handicrafts and art lined the walls of the posh club, and the *San Francisco Call*, in its January 8 issue, described the event:

The Century Club, composed of many of the most prominent literary, artistic and social women of San Francisco, was host to a large reception in its commodious clubhouse.

The rooms were filled with Indian art work and curios, until every bit of wall space, even to the windows, was covered with things that went to make up one of the most interesting and complete displays of the kind ever seen in this city.

Yesterday's public reception was what might have been termed a large and delightful aftermath of the Century Club's entertainment for its members the day before. It is a custom of the club to devote the first Wednesday of the month to art and literature, the second to science and education, and the third to practical questions. In arranging for the first regular entertainment of the new year, the committee on art and literature decided to make it strictly an Indian affair and everything was done to carry out the unique idea.

Many things were borrowed for the display. Paintings were loaned by James D. Phelan, Mrs. Louis Sloss contributed her valuable collection, Mrs. Charles Wheeler furnished a number of pictures of Indian characters painted by Mrs. Grace Hudson.

On Wednesday evening, in the midst of all these evidences of aboriginal art and character, the club held its entertainment. The program consisted of reading a number of papers prepared especially for the occasion. Mrs. Hudson discussed the Pomo tribe. After the regular program, a reception was held in honor of Mrs. Grace Hudson, the artist who makes a speciality of Indian character.

Included in the decorations for the Century Club reception was Grace's first canvas of 1897, *Let's Make Up*, number "78." The start of a new year always seemed to bring forth a canvas of exceptional size and quality from Grace's Ukiah studio. With dimensions of 28- by 38-inches, the canvas was truely a life-sized portrait of two young Indian children. Those who viewed it at the Century Club, as well as thousands more who saw it at the Mechanics Fair later in the year considered it a masterpiece.

In January, 1898, the painting found its way to a Denver showing. While there the *Denver Times* reported that a gentleman, lately arrived from Europe, was attracted by the picture and commented that no two faces which he had seen during the past year in Luxembourg or at the Louvre could compare in their line and detail with the faces of the two children seen in *Let's Make Up*.

Oftentimes, Grace Hudson's interest in her husband's ethnological activities prompted her to paint subjects which contemporaries felt were unusual or distasteful. Grace was the type of artist more concerned with the opinions of posterity than with those of her immediate audience and did not concern herself if a canvas did not please the general, picture-loving public.

Perhaps because of this, Grace attempted on several occasions to capture the spirit of the Pomo tribe in matters concerning death and funerals.

Throughout most Pomo territory, cremation was the honorable and traditional mode of disposing of the dead. Almost immediately after death, preparations were started for the burning. The body was dressed in the finest garments and ornaments that the relatives could provide, then the family, relatives, and mourning friends began to heap the corpse with *ka-ya*, the wampum bead money of the

Let's Make Up
Location Unknown

Pomo. First the mouth and hands were filled, the breast covered, and, in proportion to the deceased's popularity, the body was more or less hidden from view.

Large quantities of wood were placed in a pit two feet deep and four by five feet wide and long. The body was placed on top of the wood, which was usually stacked to a height of five or six feet. With the first blaze, the spirit of the deceased departed. The mourners marched, wailing loudly, around the fire as it burned. They sometimes sat in rows around the fire, often remaining so close as to receive burns from the intense heat. When the fire had consume the wood and body, all ashes were brushed into the pit, which was then filled with dirt. Each funeral pyre impoverished an entire clan.

By the end of the Nineteenth Century, burial customs among the Pomos had replaced their more traditional cremation. The old custom of accompanying the deceased with all of their worldly possessions, however, had not yet been abandoned. Quite frequently baskets, money beads, garments, ornaments, and priceless gifts accompanied a burial. In the case of the death of an infant, the carrying basket was buried, or on occassion was floated away down a river.

In her painting of *The Empty Basket*, number "81," Grace Hudson depicted the entire range of human emotions present at the death of a loved one, yet preserved forever the funeral procession of the Pomo tribe. An invisible light focused attention on the primary figure of the composition, suggesting the strong belief that the Indians held regarding the spirit's afterlife.

One of her strongest compositions, *The Calling of the Coyote*, number "109," illustrated the profound grief that the Indian felt at the passing of a friend. It quickly became the subject of reviews and comments:

A more ambitious work is The Calling of the Kiota *(God). Perhaps in some points it may be censured. The critics may do that. The picture has beauties which, once seen, cling in the mind and invite again to visit it. A priest (medicine man) of the American Indians, in ceremonial feathers and mystic ornaments, aged, yet stalwart, stands evoking the god to come and bear away the spirit of the dead. The dead, in this poignant picture, is a warrior lying at his feet, covered with the funeral cloth. Sitting on the ground is a young woman with dull face of ther tribe, but she is looking into the air from whence the priest prays the Kiota to come, and her eyes tell the feeling of all humanity in bereavement—the yearning for a visible sign of the Great Spirit. The head of the old "chief mourner" with a face wrinkled and full of meaning, eyes closed, perhaps blind, could hardly be excelled.*

Coming of the Coyote
Private Collection

Soon after the completion of *The Calling of the Coyote*, her first major canvas of 1898; Grace Hudson concluded her statement on the theme of Pomo death with her painting of *The Orphan*, number "113." A short inscription, titled "Da-bo-lin, The Mourning Hours," was written by the artist to accompany the painting.

At sunset there was a tribal wailing for the dead. The wail is a peculiar unison chant with words expressing unconsolable sorrow which can be heard for great distances. In my childhood in Potter Valley, it was considered a part of the day. All work eased at sunset, so they might get home in time for "Da-bo-lin." All Indians are sad in the evening and those who have griefs grieve most then.

The name of the dead is never spoken. If he was named for anything, a tree, flower or bird, the name of it was changed in that tribe forever. The grandmother will not mention the mother's name to the child, but they understand.

The Orphan was exhibited at the Trans-Mississippi International Exposition at Omaha, Nebraska, and at the Mechanics Fair in San Francisco, where it received a cash prize.

The Orphan also revealed that Grace did not hesitate to alter her own work. In the 17 years between A. O. Carpenter's 1898 photograph of the completed painting and its sale, Grace reworked her subject to alter many details, if not the major elements of the composition. A *San Francisco Chronicle* article on December 12, 1915, contained the line, "Sadness is in the woman's face, while the child uplifts its face almost questioningly." The child's eyes, closed in 1898, had been opened by 1915. Many other changes of detail may be found when the two versions are closely compared.

. . . . .

Hogs
Private Collection

Only eight years had passed since Grace Hudson had commenced painting the California Indians, an activity that had grown to become a lifetime calling. Her subjects had grown in number until they spanned nearly the entire Pomo community of Ukiah, and she had won their full confidence and friendship. With a great deal of pride, they would say to visitors, "Grace Hudson, our friend, she all same us." When Grace arrived at the rancheria with her sketch pad or oftentimes just to visit, the children frequently would announce her arrival with joyful shouts of "The Painter Lady is here!"

She was often consulted on the choice of the appropriate English name for a new baby, and frequently suggested the names of her San Francisco friends, with their permission. Greenie, for example, was named in honor of Charles S. Green, editor of the *Overland Monthly*.

Among the Indians painted by Grace Hudson in the last years of the Nineteenth Century were Old Captain Bill, the chief of the Yokaya tribe, Burman, Dr. Hudson Billy Bow-legs, Jennie's Tom, and others. Many of the above group were the subject of more than one painting. The chubby-cheeked Burman, for example, provided a subject for more than eight of Grace's works.

Many of these paintings were produced as miniature canvases. Seven works which she finished in 1897, for example, were smaller in length than six inches. Often, these were prepared under commission for a client who wanted "some little thing" done by the now-famous artist.

The frequent comment, "She must paint with a magnifying glass," was often heard when gallery visitors first viewed Hudson miniatures; indeed, she did. The smallest of her paintings was as perfect in detail as her largest, suggesting to some that viewing the works with a magnifying glass was the only way to fully appreciate her skill.

Among the subjects that she treated as miniatures were basket babies in the tradition of *Little Mendocino*, infants with dogs, and children's portraits. Also included with her tiny canvases is perhaps the most whimsical and unusual Hudson subject, *Hogs*, number "99." Any doubt that the artist had a sense of humor about her work vanished with the completion of this six-inch, round painting.

To Grace Hudson, her art had become not only a vocation, but was now also an avocation. While she was capable of exerting the intense study due a masterpiece, many casual and delightful paintings appeared that seemed to have been created for her own personal enjoyment. They differed from her serious, major works as the orchestra's practice session might vary from a concert, or the athlete's warm-up stands apart from his game.

Although Grace and John Hudson were never blessed with a child of their own, Grace must have received a great deal of satisfaction in painting the children of her Pomo friends. Hardly a month passed that she did not have one or another Indian infant tightly laced in a carrying basket or crawling naked before her easel. If her subjects had been nobility and the paintings works commissioned by European royalty, few museums, courts, or castles would have been without a Hudson portrait hanging in a place of honor. She had become one of the most accomplished western artists in the country.

CHAPTER 5

TRAVELS AND A NEW CENTURY

Travels to Hawaii, Chicago, and Europe

THE FIRST YEAR of the new century was for Grace Hudson, one of miniatures. Grace was rapidly approaching the median of her life, and the intense concentration which her profession demanded was beginning to take its toll. Nearly two-thirds of the paintings completed during 1900 had demensions less than eight inches, and only three were larger than 18 inches. Still, her output for the year totaled 30 new oils.

As was her custom, the first canvas of the year was a major work. Titled *The Whispering Leaves* and numbered "155," it portrayed a young girl from the Mendocino coastal village of Westport, sitting among the dry leaves of the autumn forest. Her composition was based on an ancient Indian legend of the Pomos.

The Pomos believed that there was one day in the year when the trees of the forest had the power of speech, a day in October when the dry leaves whispered as they fluttered to the ground. The day was a time to pause, listen to the leaves, and reflect. In the rustle of the falling foliage, the old and weary sought commendation, the young men and women desired encouragement and assurance, and the children, who were told that wonderful things could be promised those who had been good, waited as the shadows lengthened and stillness once more returned to the woods.

Whispering Leaves was exhibited for several months in 1900 at the Oakland Public Library, where it was evidently a favorite of the library patrons. On April 15, 1900 the *Oakland Tribune* reported:

The most recent change in the collection has been the taking away of Mrs. Grace Hudson's charming painting of the little Indian girl listening to The Whispering Leaves. *The picture, while it was with us, attracted great attention and many people came to see it again and again. We of the library became much attached to it and were sorry to see it go. It went to a city where one of Mrs. Hudson's patrons wished to look at it and it was his picture as soon as he saw it. Oakland again certainly hopes to be favored with some of Mrs. Hudson's canvases. She has made so close a study of the Mendocino Indians that her work has special value and charm.*

Most of the miniature canvases of 1900 were intended to fill the insatiable demand for her works which had grown in the art public. Even as she worked, Grace increasingly sought respite from the strict routine of her studio. When the hop season began, the "Painter Lady," as the Pomo's now called her, visited the summer camps along the Russian River, prepared to record another aspect of the lives of the local Indians. *The Diplomat*, number "162," resulted from her stay.

The Whispering Leaves
Private Collection

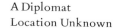

A Diplomat
Location Unknown

Home Care
Location Unknown

John and Grace Hudson frequently joined campers and outdoorsmen in visiting the countryside near Ukiah. In July and August, the pair usually traveled to the Mendocino coast, their trip timed to coincide with the peak of the hunting season or the ripening of wild berries along the shoreline. But the summer of 1900 provided a more ambitious trip for the Hudsons.

Joining their lifetime friend, Pearl Fine, they journeyed on July 27 to Yosemite Valley to camp out in the splendor of majestic granite cliffs and thundering waterfalls. The scenery at Yosemite had already been recorded by Thomas Ayres, Albert Bierstadt, Thomas Hill, as well as a score of more minor artists, and no Hudson canvases are known to have resulted from her visit. People, not inanimate landscapes, were her forte.

Returning to her studio, Grace once again resumed work. As the California State Fair of 1900 approached, she prepared a canvas of special quality. Titled *Home Care*, and numbered "172," it scored a success with the judges, who awarded it a cash prize. The subject of the painting was Myrt, a young girl. She not only endeared herself to the fairgoers, but her portrait found a special place in the heart of William S. Hopkins, a member of the Stanford University faculty. It was a treasure that Hopkins enjoyed for more than 30 years, for after that period of time, Grace replied to his letter of inquiry:

It is gratifying to hear from one who has lived so long with one of my little Indians, and still loves her. I feel it a very fine compliment.

Thirty years ago we did not realize that the Indian would not be with us always and I did not keep so careful a record as I do now. However, in my notes is "Myrt with pedah, 30 x 18½, painted in 1900." The number would be on the back of the canvas. Pedah is the Indian doll, a stick with wampum eyes.

I recall my friendship with little Myrt. Her father and mother had separated, the mother returning to her people in Lake County. She heard Monk [her husband] was dying and, taking Myrt on her back, walked from Upper Lake to Ukiah, thirty miles. Here she came to me for news and assistance for the remaining eight miles. I saw a great deal of Myrt that summer.

Monk did not die. He was the leader of the dancers many years.

I have sailed many seas since then. The Indians from the rancheria have died or scattered. Myrt had disappeared.

Like many other artists, Grace had involved herself so deeply in the lives and customs of her subjects that she had grown too close to the Pomos. Many of the canvases completed in the past two years were mere restatements of themes that the artist had already successfully recorded, technically perfect yet somehow lacking the spark of genius that had propelled her to the forefront of Western Art. She desperately needed rest and relaxation.

For much of the time, John was away from Ukiah. His collecting activities had grown far beyond the level of an amateur's interest. He frequently traveled up and down the state to gather Indian artifact and record the customs of the coastal tribes. His collection eventually drew the attention of the curators of the Field Museum of Chicago and resulted in an appointment to the official position of collector of the institution. Although he welcomed the responsibilities that his new status demanded, his duties further separated him from Grace.

There were many resort facilities near Ukiah, but Grace Hudson recognized in herself the need to leave behind the familiar places and people of northern California. For the first time since 1891, the paint on her palette and brushes was allowed to dry. Packing her belongings into steamer trunks, she sailed alone for the Hawaiian Islands.

The *Pacific Commercial Advertiser*, a Honolulu newspaper, reported January 7, 1901:

Mrs. Grace Hudson, a painter of Indian subjects, is at the Hawaiian Hotel. Her visit to Hawaii is purely one of rest and recreation and she professes herself as being so charmed with the dolce far niente life, with the fragrant breezes and the many-changing scenes of interest in Honolulu that her brief stay may be prolonged indefinitely, in order to regain that health and strength for which the trip was originally undertaken. Later on Mrs. Hudson will travel leisurely through both Tahiti and Samoa. It is Mrs. Hudson's intention to paint Hawaiian juvenile life, as she had done Indian youth. She does her pictures from life and from photographs, the latter enabling her to get poses too ephemeral for painting from the real.

By birth Mrs. Hudson is a Californian and from Mendocino County. Potter Valley, her home, which also the home of the Pomo tribe of Indians, and as a young girl she had ample opportunity to study her subjects and through her knowledge of their mode of life and habits she has attained a popular success.

Her painting of a Pomo child at the Paris Exposition received honorable mention and her Crying Baby *was on exhibition at the World's Fair in 1893.* Little Mendocino *attracted great attention and* Mamma *was exhibited at the San Francisco Press Club, of which Mrs. Hudson is an honorary member.*

Captain John, *the chief of the Pomos, is now in the possession of the National Museum at Washinton, D. C. She has had canvases exhibited in London, Paris, New York, Chicago and San Francisco, as well as many other large cities.*

While her first days in the islands were spent in restful relaxation, Grace did, in time attempt to sketch and paint. The result of these efforts, however, were less than successful. John Hudson, meanwhile, had left Ukiah for Chicago and the Field Museum where he concentrated on cataloguing his extensive collection of California Indian artifacts.

The correspondence between the couple throughout the time of their separation revealed much of their personal feelings toward one another, Grace's despair at her inability to paint successfully, and a few insights into their relationships with other friends. Grace wrote, on February 10, 1901:

I can hardly imagine the cold weather you are having in Chicago. We are having rain but it is warm enough to use a fan. Staying indoors makes me almost homesick until I think of Ukiah and the scattered condition of the Hudson family and their belongings . . . I am feeling very well only I cannot sleep enough. Please tell me something to do. I fall asleep as soon as I get in bed then awaken about four and and sleep no more. Night after night. Sometimes I get a short nap during the day, but not often. I tried to paint a little last week, but the same old tired feeling came back so I put away the paints and will go on resting; if only I could sleep . . . Good night, Johnnie boy, you cannot imagine how much I miss you.

A few weeks later, she again took pen in hand to write John Hudson:

. . . The weather is cool and pleasant though I still get tired easily. I weighed 103 pounds this morning. I wonder if I am getting rested mentally. I feel as though I never want to paint again. I hate the sight of my brushes so will go on frolicking for a time . . .

Finally, on March 12, 1901, she reported:

My desire to paint has returned. I had a model and worked hard today. A young girl with lais. I think I will rent a studio and paint for a month anyway. I would be ashamed to go back with nothing . . . You ask if I am ever homesick, yes and no. I long to see you but I am not homesick for Ukiah. I could not live there without you and I cannot think of any place I would rather be alone than here.

John Hudson's letters, though more infrequent than Grace's, provided additional insights. After returning from Chicago, he wrote:

At this hour eleven years ago there was a little ceremony in Ukiah in which we were primas and tonight finds me looking back to that occasion and its sequel. I find many things in myself to condemn, my want of affection or its exhibition, my indifference to the future and want of energy to reach an ideal for both of us. I cannot account for much of this; though from the experience of my last four months of earnest, almost happy work, I can believe that my old profession was a master I secretly abhorred and had not the courage to leave.

Perhaps, I am premature in conclusions, but I believe that when our home arrangements are settled to our mutual satisfaction that I will be perfectly happy and pursue a life that may result in honor and money consideration.

You have worked too hard, my dear, in these past years and I see no reason for its repetition as long as we live. I forget what sum you have stored away, but its interest with what sales you may make in the future should supply you with pin money. I don't want you to quit painting but it should be not for revenue only, but for pleasure and honor.

By June, Grace had begun to work in earnest. The *Pacific Commercial Advertiser* reported on June 7, 1901:

Mrs. Grace Hudson, California's famous artist, who has been sojourning for the past three months in Honolulu, declares herself a victim to the charms of Hawaii, and has determined to remain in the Island indefinitely.

She has taken up her painting and finds the Hawaiian, Japanese and Chinese children of Honolulu's cosmopolitan population so attractive from a standpoint of art work that she intends opening a studio and devoting her attention to Island types. From the splendid sketches that have already come from her hands, made during her vacation here, it is safe to predict that the famous little artist whose reproductions of Indian juveniles of Mendocino County have occasioned comment and praise from art critics in France and England, as well as all over the United States, will make an equal success of her paintings of the small specimens of Hawaiian humanity. . .

"I have been idling long enough," said the ambitious little woman last night in an interview, "and I feel that I must get to work in real earnest. I am going to Hilo instead of remaining here because they tell me it is so much easier to get models over there. Do you know, I have had the hardest work getting models? They run away from me. I used to kidnap my little papooses when I painted the Ukiah Indians, but I find that difficult here. They will come once, and promise to sit for me again, but they don't return, and how can I find them? When I ask them where they live, they make a wide sweep of the arm that may mean anywhere from Diamond Head to Punch Bowl, and so I can't go after them and bring them here to my rooms in the hotel. When I get settled in Hilo, I will live right next door to them, as it were, and I will just reach out and get them, or paint them in their homes. I have no scruples about stealing infants, and have done it many times. Once I get hold of them, I can manage them pretty well, by means of gumdrops

and that kind of thing. I think there is great opportunity for an artist here in the Islands; there is no place like it for coloring. I do not, as a rule, however, paint landscape. I have found a great opportunity in the Hawaiian children.

By mid-August, it was announced in the *Pacific Commercial Advertiser* that the visiting California painter who had been plying her brushes at Hilo for two months was returning to Honolulu with a number of sketches which she had commenced on the other island. She intended to finish her art in the city. Grace Hudson was met at the wharf by her friends.

Throughout the city of Honolulu, anticipation grew of Grace's efforts at painting portraits of the colorful island residents. Finally, in the *Evening Bulletin* of Honolulu of October 18, 1901, a small, commercial exhibition was announced.

Three paintings by Mrs. G. Hudson, placed in the Pacific Hardware Co.'s window this morning, attracted a great deal of attention and elicited general admiration. Two of them are small canvases, each representing a Hawaiian girl at home. The third is a good-sized picture, showing a young Hawaiian girl eating poi by herself. She is sitting on a cocoanut-leaf mat, taking part of her weight on her left hand. The forefinger of her right hand is placing a lift of the native pottage in her mouth. There is in the countenance, fringed with heavy tresses, the archly sky expression characteristic of Hawaiian maidenhood. While the live figure is itself portrayed with an art seldom seen equalled with Hawaiian subjects, the accessories are laid with a perfection of coloring which absolutely forbids all adverse criticism. The calico drapery of the girl, the cracked calabash with its light patch in the rich dark wood, the dried squid lying near the vessel, the weave of the mat and the clusters of taro plant leaves—all reveal a wonderfully deft handling of shades and delicate tints. There was just one objection heard on the outside. It was by a local pundit in native customs. He declared that the Hawaiians never place the calabash on the floor mat, but the vessel must rest upon its individual mat.

Mary Lou Eating Poi
Location Unknown

Altogether, in the months between January and November, Grace Hudson completed 27 paintings of the Hawaiian people. Most were small oil sketches, one a diminutive three inches wide by four inches tall *Mary Lou Eating Poi*, number "196," and described above, received the most praise and comment.

. . . . .

Dr. Hudson's love for Grace, his written claims of loneliness, and his professed desire for her companionship when he returned to Chicago finally drew the artist back from the surf and palms of Hawaii. On November 16, 1901, she docked in San Francisco aboard the *S. S. China*. Two days later, she and the doctor left by train for Chicago for what amounted to their second honeymoon.

Her brief passage through San Francisco had enabled her to place a number of her paintings at the local galleries, where they prompted fresh praise for Grace. The *San Francisco Chronicle* described her new paintings:

Grace Hudson is the first American artist of note to bring something worthwhile from the Hawaiian Islands. No one could be better fitted for the mission, no one could have gone in a more sympathetic or intelligent spirit. For years in California Mrs. Hudson has studied the Indian life until she knows and can express the languour that lies in the eye of semi-civilization and the texture of the soft, dark skin. Her studies of the redmen have brought Mrs. Hudson fame, and she has added to it by the many paintings of the island folk now on exhibition in the Rabjohn Ken-

nedy Gallery.

This interesting collection is the result of several months' stay among the natives of the Hawaiian Islands. Mrs. Hudson had to journey to the out-of-the-way places to get the best subjects; she had to linger among the people until they learned to know her and until they were quite at their ease.

The largest and one of the most important of Mrs. Hudson's pictures she calls A Kamaaina. *In this a native child, frowsy-headed and bright-eyed, is kneeling in ecstasy over a calabash of poi from which she is eating with her finger, after the fashion of the most-approved table manners of the Hawaiians. The child and the feast are on a rug of matting and in the background taro is growing, the succulent, big, glossy leaves telling the remainder of the story of the national dish.*

With many people, the heads of a half-white Hawaiian woman and a full-blooded boy will be given first place. Mrs. Hudson put the dusky, fine-eyed beauty against a light background and over her shapely figure drew a plain white fichu of soft material, bringing out the warm beauty of the fine brown skin in strong relief. The head of the boy is done in a deeper tone, but an equally effective one. A native child sitting on a beach is one of excellent portrayal of child life. Several small oils are exquisite in drawing and treatment. One of the best of these is called Punahele, *the Hawaiian name for chums. In this a pretty native child is holding two kittens, one sprawled over each arm. In another a native girl is decorated with the leis of flowers and in still another there is a dark missie, happy in the possession of a lei made in imitation of those wrought in the costly feathers possessed by royalty.*

Whether due to the anticipation of a Chicago summer, completion of the work of unpacking, cleaning, sorting, identifying, cataloguing, and displaying the hundreds of Indian artifacts previously collected and shipped to the Field Museum by Dr. Hudson, or merely the effect of simple homesickness, the couple traveled west, arriving at Ukiah on May 16, 1902. In every way, Grace and her husband had been strengthened by their separation of nearly one year.

After a few weeks becoming settled, Grace again took up her brushes. Placing blank canvas on her easel, she once more began to paint. The result was one of the finest paintings of the entire Hudson collection, *The Dowry,* number "212." Mary Loff Mitchell, posing in the attire of a Pomo bride, was the subject. The finest kind of baskets and the most precious sorts of shells and feathered jewelry completed the young bride's trousseau array.

The Dowry was a popular success as well. When it was exhibited at the California State Fair of 1902, it was awarded a cash prize.

Gone from Grace Hudson was the nervous need to paint constantly. During the next year, from June, 1902 until June, 1903, Grace accompanied John Hudson on many of his anthropological outings. Some of her old friends and subjects, Tullo, Annie and Willum, were remembered in small portraits, and she prepared three canvases of Shoshone Indian children from Tijon, California. In all just eight paintings were completed by the end of 1902.

If any of the art patrons of the United States had forgotten the petite, blonde artist during her absence, they were alerted to her return by both newspapers and magazines which featured her in their issues. The August, 1902 issue of *Western Field* magazine, in its premiere edition, published a full-page article, titled "A California Expert." The expert was none other than Grace Hudson. A photograph revealed her, wearing the latest in women's sports apparel, holding a huge trout.

The same journal, in its September issue, carried a four page illustrated article entitled, "Some Good Indians," by an author with the unlikely name of Sobanichi. The story indicated the grudging credit given a painter of Indians at the turn of the

The Dowery
Private Collection

century, as well as illustrating the prejudices still evident regarding the Native Americans themselves.

An eminent authority defines Art as the interpretation of natural impressions through individual temperament. If that be true, Creation has dealt very kindly with one Western artist, blessing her with a temperament at once sweetly poetic, kindly sympathetic, idealistic to the degree of a loveable fault, and, yet almost ascetic to its devotion to truthful detail and rigid precision.

Were I to be asked to nominate America's most conscientious artist, I would unhesitantly name Grace Hudson. There is an integrity about her work, which, diamond-like, is self-illumined by its own inherent purity. There is, likewise, an engaging extension of this rare characteristic to the personality of the woman herself. One is impressed, even on first contact, as much with the sincerity of purpose and loyalty to her art, as with her sweet gentleness and rare courtesy, even to indifferent strangers. Frank, unaffected and fairly devoid of the class egotism usually born of great success, she is charming type of the higher Western Evolution—a loveable genius because she is a purely womanly one.

In her one agreeably misses the mannerisms of the guild, the pose and patois of the shop. She talks English understandably and is addicted to the heresy of a genuine laugh. Though dainty as a bit of Khasmi gauze, she is wholly tangible and shakes hands with a firm grip, after the fashion of all healthy, hardworking enthusiasts.

Best of all, she has a fine estimate of her own ability and full confidence in her own powers. "My Indians," she says, with a nice arrogance, and, listening to her proud intonation of it, one irresistibly cedes the claim. It is the more easy because no other living artist even approximates to the Hudson type. Her Indians are truely and distinctively her very own! . . .

Her good Indians assuredly look prettier than the sort we used to find a certain beatitude in making, and have, besides, a large intrinsic value. We old-school artists lacked her exquisite refinement of motif, as well as her wondrous delicacy of treatment; and our moral perspective was not as good. Yet our work was always essentially in drawing—it had to be, for on that one canon of art depended the whole result. We drew fine and first, for obvious reasons. All our work was of the impressionistic type, and we took care to make the impressions deep.

To conclude a proverbially odious comparison, let me but add that Mrs. Hudson's Indians enjoy one distinction that we cannot claim for ours—they have invariably been "hung on the line . . . " [This phrase refers to canvases hung at an exhibition.]

Considering the precariously short step from the artistic to the commonplace, the genius of Mrs. Hudson is sharply accentuated in her pictures . . .

Naturally her greatest success has been attained in her child pictures. For, next to herself, a normal woman loves babies better than anything else on earth and only a woman can understand and interpret a baby's inchoate emotions, especially an Indian baby with its immobile, grease-sweating face and unfathomable eyes, which mock at all your conclusions . . .

The writer continued, more unkindly:

. . . The almost painful faithfulness of her rendering evidences close and conscientious study, but is work thrown away. She attempts to justify it by saying that she is painting futurity and aims at ethnological value, forgetting that, in matters of prosaic details of value only to ethnologists, the camera can do even more severely accurate work in a fraction of the time and expense and without any waste of precious talent and nervous energy. Even Grace Hudson cannot put

soul into a trashy basket or frowsy serape, despite their all too usual animation.

Grace Hudson has enjoyed the uninterrupted success and fame, her work being invariably hung on the line wherever exhibited.

To the credit of Californian good taste and judgment, be it said: but little of her work ever gets out of the state, the best examples being jealously snatched up by local admirers before completion . . .

It is the penalty of genius to be criticized and sex is no exemption. Genius owes an incontrovertable obligation to its generation and we have the entailed right to ask for something more serious from the pencil of Grace Hudson. One does not expect landscapes from her, for she evidently cannot paint a background. Her forte is especially genre *and California is one great oyster full of pearls ready for the opening with her palette knife. Whether she has the courage to attempt it is another question. It is so hard to get out of a rut—especially when it is comfortably lubricated by the material unction which always attends upon popular success.*

Whatever her motive, Grace Hudson must have felt a need to return to her easel, for in 1903 and 1904, a total of 42 paintings emerged from the studio in Ukiah. With an extended vacation in the Hawaiian Islands, a second honeymoon trip to Chicago, and her travels with John up and down the state of California now behind her, the lady artist once more explored the Pomo tribe for subject matter, concentrating most of her effort on the Mitchell, Duncan, and Peters families. These were the Pomos who considered Grace "my folk;" she knew their every mood and expression. A new group of Pomo offspring had populated the rancheria since Grace had left in January, 1901. The result was an outpouring of fresh subject matter from her brushes. In only a few short months, the gallery walls of San Francisco were filled with quizzical brown eyes peering out at passing art admirers.

As before her travels to Hawaii, John found himself drawn from Ukiah by his duties for the Field Museum. On February 26, 1904, the *Ukiah Republican Press* noted:

Dr. Hudson left last week for Albuquerque, New Mexico, where he will meet with Dr. Dorsey, the general superintendent of the Field Museum in Chicago. Dr. Hudson has been collecting baskets and other artifacts manufactured by the Indians of the Pacific slopes for this museum for sometime past. Each year a man and a woman from twelve tribes are taken to Albuquerque, so that the different tribal customs and arts may be studied and their work exhibited.

When Grace was not busy painting, she would lend a hand to John, assisting him with his work. Early in 1905, the pair traveled east once more, to Chicago. Grace must have left Ukiah with a portfolio full of sketches or a trunk packed with canvases in need of finishing touches, for the first nine months of that year added 26 new Hudsons to her already lengthy series.

Grace Hudson had now been copyrighting her paintings for several years, and it now was possible to identify not only the year of completion of her new canvases, but also the month and day of filing. The artist was always generous with her paintings and had often consented to their reproduction in print, but the paintings had become a source of income for the postcard industry. She found it necessary to protect the interests of her patrons by copyrighting the finished works. Many of the copyright records are still on file at the Library of Congress, though most have long since expired.

While John and Grace were in Chicago, they were visited by friends from

Ukiah, Mr. and Mrs. J. C. Ruddocks. After being guests in the Hudson house for a short time, they wrote to the Ukiah *Republican Press* to share their experiences with its readers:

The Doctor has become an expert on the Indian, his habits, customs, tradition, implements, general mode of living and history. He has charge of the anthropological department, comprehending the American Indian. He has been collecting relics, dresses, weapons, foods and implements, and is allotted the task of classifying and cataloguing all the articles in that section of the museum. Some of the immensity of this great exhibit can be formed when one learns that there are eight miles of show cases in the portion under Dr. Hudson's supervision. One can see here everything relating to the Indian life, from the war-like Sioux to the indolent Pomo.

In the fall of 1905, Grace Hudson wiped the paint from her brushes again and shipped all the finished canvases back to San Francisco art dealers. John turned in his key to the Field Museum, and the two prepared to depart the city of Chicago. This time, instead of retracing their path westward to Ukiah, they embarked on an extended tour of Europe.

For Grace and John, the trip was strictly a vacation. It was a time to see the world, or at least another part of it. Any suggestion that Grace used the travels to study art in Europe would be erroneous, for if any studying was done, it was with the aid of a Baedeker tour guide.

Included in their itinerary were Scotland, England, Holland, France, Germany, Austria, Switzerland, and Italy. Their first stop was Edinburgh.

Edinburgh is old, romantic and beautiful. The city is on hills topped by great castles. We visited St. Giles Cathedral, have seen where heads were chopped off, kings born, and found it hard to believe that such wicked people could have built such beautiful structures.

We visited both Sir Walter Scott's and Robert Burns' homes. Wondered at the art collections of the Royal Scottish Academy, the Royal Scottish Museum and the National Gallery of Scotland. Never enough time to really see them . . .

We attended one event where the chairman publicly thanked Professor Hudson for honoring them with his presence. We were awfully puffed up. We have enjoyed the people tremendously. They are charming, delightful and courteous, as well as being the soul of human kindness.

From England, they wrote again.

We have seen palaces and cathedrals so numerous that it is impossible to describe them. Father would so enjoy seeing them, but I doubt if you could stand the tramping, spiral stairways and the cold wind . . .

Our accomodations have been quaint. The little old-fashioned hotel where we are staying comes with a landlady that asks us what we wish for each meal and when we wish it served . . .

London, how I wish you could see just one of these buildings. The Library of Congress is cheap and taudy in comparison. The size and grandeur of Westminster Abbey is beyond words. We have visited the Tower, seen the spot where Anne Bolen, Queen Catherine Howard, Lady Jane Grey were beheaded, stood on their graves and patted the tombs of a long line of monarchs . . .

The November weather is cold and wet and so are the houses. They are heated (if you could call it that) by a little grate fire about the size of a sugar bowl. John was afraid to throw a grape skin on the fire, lest he put it out . . .

During their stay in Paris, the fourth stop on their tour, the couple visited the Louvre and the palace at Versailles. From France, they traveled to the German cities of Cologne and Heidelberg, then passed into Austria at Strasburg. The pace of their travels was beginning to tire them out, and in Switzerland they took a welcome retreat from their journey.

We have spent the day loitering and doing as the spirit move us and it has been a great success. Sometimes we get tired of Baedeker and seeing the things we should. In a place like this, the attraction is the setting . . . With such quaint architecture and such medieval atmosphere, it is just fun to wander and discover for ourselves . . .

By the time we return, I shall be able to say "hot" in every language in Europe. It often takes all of them, plus a few adjectives, to even get a cup of luke warm coffee.

We are somewhat rested now, after three splendid days in Geneva. One day we slept in until 11 o'clock—shame! The lake has the clearest water I have ever seen. We can see every pebble on the bottom and watch the little ducks in the privacy of their diving. Every city has swans and we joined the rest of the people in the enjoyment of feeding them . . .

In Cologne we paid a franc to see three thorns from the crown Jesus wore, a piece of the true cross, a scrap of the blood-stained garment of John the Baptist, and a piece of linen in which the infant Jesus was wrapped. With all this, plus the riches of the cathedrals, you would probably feel sorry for John, knowing how I have to sit on him to keep him subdued at such exhibitions . . .

We received your news of Charmian's marriage. Jack London did very well. If anything can boost him higher, she certainly can . . .

January of 1906 found the Hudsons in Italy, experiencing the grandeur of Florence and the coolness of Venice. Then they turned their footsteps south to the Italian capital.

Rome! We thought we were busy seeing things before, but Rome makes you feel that you have only just begun. I could hardly sleep the first night after we arrived, for thinking over the wonders. Poor John, I hurry him from morning until night. He complains that he is being rushed through Europe with no time to see anything. I feel as though we would never get home if he does not move more promptly . . .

The Hudson plans had originally included a visit to Egypt and the Middle East, but by the end of January, chronic travel fatigue had set in. The trip to Egypt was cancelled, and the couple traveled to Naples, Pompeii, and Mount Vesuvius. From Naples, a final letter was sent to Ukiah.

My head is bursting with what I have tried to put in it. Tomorrow we leave for Naples and from there we will sail for New York. Anyway, it is time to tell the people in the studio to be moving. John wants to go to Spain, but my head has shut up shop. It is a shame to go when you cannot enjoy it . . .

On February 21, 1906, they were aboard the *SS Republic White Star*, billed to reach New York City on March 5.

We have 44 first-class passengers, 200 second-class and 2,240 steerages. Including a crew of 200, it would equal all of Ukiah in one big boat, and with room to spare. I do not know how the steerage passengers manage. You can hardly believe the number of people that are pouring into the United States aboard every ship. We are certainly getting the poor, the tired and the hungry masses . . .

We cannot tell exactly when we will get home. It is possible that we may go by way of Washington. I want a little time in San Francisco for new arrangements with Schussler. We will stop at the California Hotel.

It will be so wonderful to be home.

CHAPTER 6

BACK TO CALIFORNIA

New Canvases of the Pomo

T HE HUDSONS returned to California, where they found San Francisco in ruins. On April 18, 1906, the catastrophic earthquake and fire in the Bay Area had killed over 450 persons and destroyed more than 25,000 buildings. Perhaps worse, the calamity took a heavy toll of Hudson canvases. At Schussler's gallery, the Press Club, numerous private homes, and business offices her paintings were burned, slashed by falling stone and plaster, or otherwise damaged. Grace's notebook grimly recorded:

Number 29, burned at the Press Club, number 69 injured by falling glass in earthquake, number 82 burned in St. Francis Hotel, number 139 burned at the California Hotel, number 147 burned in Santa Rosa, number 148 burned at Schussler Bros; numbers 158, 161, 170, 190, 211, 266, 288 all befell to similar fates.

There may have been other losses that were never reported to the artist.

From San Francisco, the couple returned to Ukiah. Tired from their travels, they were ready to relax, preserve momentos of the trip in albums, and share their European experiences with friends.

Grace had long since established her reputation in the art world. Women all over the United States were beginning to be recognized for their achievements in many fields that previously had been exclusively male. For the first time, a woman rode in an airplane, women were elected as members of the American Society of Engineers and other professional organizations, and a nurse was appointed to a university professorship. It was a period of readjustment and change from more traditional values.

Even though Grace returned to her easel, only half of the 16 paintings which she produced in 1906 had dimensions larger than ten inches.

Early in March, one of her 1898 canvases, *Tom with a Jack Rabbit*, number "116," was singled out for the cover design of *Western Field* magazine. About the painting, the editor wrote:

The striking picture which serves as a cover design for this month's issue is a purposely rough-engraved enlargement of a miniature photograph of one of Mrs. Grace Hudson's splendid Indian paintings, kindly loaned to us by her for the purpose of reproduction. Realizing the utter impossibility of faithfully reproducing in printer's ink the exquisitely life-like coloring and living flesh effects of the

Tom with Jack Rabbit
Location Unknown

original, we preferred to utilize it in the manner shown, as any attempt to offer it in colors would be a positive injustice to this famous artist and her work.

It may be of interest to our readers to know that Mrs. Hudson is and has been for some time abroad, enjoying the galleries of the old masters throughout Europe. It is doubtful, however, if the old world will yield her anything but comparisons, for her style is uniquely her own and her drawing, composition and handling of color are not excelled by any painter, living or dead.

Perhaps the most significant painting of the year was *The Candy Boy*, number "298." In the composition, Garland Mitchell is clad in a pink shirt fastened with a brass safety pin and he wears a single piece of "Indian gold," or wampum, as a pendant around his neck. The three-quarters length portrait received a silver medal at the Alaska-Yukon Exposition.

The Dove Place
Private Collection

The year also saw the completion of *Ma-yu-ma, The Dove Garden*, number "289." Eight years later Grace Hudson would again paint a similar scene, on canvas "492." During the summer and fall, the banks of the Russian River usually saw a convergence of doves and Indians. Both came to the waterway for the same purpose: gathering the seeds of the tarweed plants which grew along the dry riverbed. *Ma-yu-ma* portrays a Pomo maiden sharing her harvest of tarweed seeds with a flock of trusting birds.

By 1907, Grace Hudson stood nearly at the halfway point in her career. As she marked the occasion of her 42nd birthday, she had achieved an enviable reputation. Gone, however, was the drive that often accompanies the quest for status within one's chosen work. The number of canvases she produced per year now frequently averaged less than 20, as compared to the 30 or more which she had finished earlier in her career. She was still very much in demand by art patrons, and articles about her still appeared in newspapers and magazines. The arrival of any of her new works in the galleries was always reported.

Two major Hudson exhibitions were held in California in 1907. The first took place at the Schussler Gallery in San Francisco, while later in the year a show was arranged at the Gould Gallery in Los Angeles.

On April 29, 1907, the *San Francisco Call Bulletin* commented:

Grace Hudson's exhibition at Schussler's will continue to the middle of this week. It would be difficult to imagine anything more deliciously quaint than some of the tiny Indian maidens she has painted. There is one called Among the Poppies *showing a little girl standing in a sea of waving poppies. Another, called* Basket Picnic, *is the picture of a girl carrying a Pomo basket of apples and fortifying herself for crossing a stream by taking a bite big enough to last her to the other side. Again, there is a tiny Indian child looking fearful at a jay, supposed to be a bird of ill omen, sitting on the branch of a tree above. The artist's gift for choosing interesting situations is as great as her ability to catch the varying expressions in the chubby brown faces and big dark eyes. The great variety of her pictures of Indian children may be due partly to the fact that she does not confine herself to one model, but is always on the lookout for good subjects. Indians are the most difficult of all people to approach, but Mrs. Hudson in her home in Ukiah has used her opportunity of making friends with them to great advantage. She makes it a point to be very faithful in her picturing of the dress and household belongings of the Indians.*

On November 9, 1907, the *Los Angeles Express* published an article on the Gould Gallery showing of Grace Hudson's work, titled, "Indian Children Shown on Canvas."

Within the past few years, the Indian has been a favorite theme for many artists, the redmen seemingly having a fascination for the artists—and on canvas for a large number of persons who would otherwise despise the none-too-fastidious descendants of the people who first inhabited the land which we call our own.

Warriors, camp scenes and many other phases of the Indian life have been depicted, but few have attempted the Indian children. Children are always difficult to paint, but more especially the half-timid and wholly afraid children of the redmen in the presence of strangers.

Grace Hudson, however, has been very successful, and has sent four charming studies of this too-little-known phase of Indian life to Los Angeles. They are hung in the Gould Gallery.

Mrs. Hudson has portrayed the children as they are among themselves, the little ones who love their dolls, their dogs and the flowers as much as the children of whiter skin.

Little Pa-dah, hugging closely his crude doll, a tradition of the Pomo Indians from time immemorial, is a brown-faced little garland with big, wondering eyes. This painting has in it a vast amount of feeling and a fine technique. The little flannel gown, with its blue and white check and but a bit of pink, is a fine piece of brush work, clear and distinct without being hard. The texture of the cloth is rather suggested than worked out. The face and head are portrait studies, and the doll, for which the child evidently cares so much, is but a piece of board with wampum eyes, and a bit of cloth wrapped around its uncompromising hard lines for a dress.

This painting is of interest historically, for, while the Indians have to a more-or-less degree adopted the customs of the white man, their children's dolls remain the same as before the advent of the Anglo-Saxon race to these shores. The only difference is in the dress, cloth substituting the earlier dress of grass.

Ho-y, the Indian word for a baby in a basket, shows tiny William Peters watching two birds singing on a branch.

Pa-tham (flowers) shows a little Pomo Indian child from Point Arena standing in a field of lupins. It lends a rather decorative scene with the subdued background color in contrast with the child's white shirt. The orange in her hand was not only to add color to the portrait, but was a necessity in order to capture the pose.

E-nach, which means "in hiding," is a little child with her dog. This painting shows . . . the peculiar laugh of the Indian, which resembles crying almost as much as laughter.

This is the first time that Mrs. Hudson has exhibited any of her Indian studies in Los Angeles. They should prove most interesting.

Engaged
Private Collection

Grace Hudson's particular talent combined an understanding of the simple joys of childhood with an ability to sensitively capture it on canvas. She somehow divined the thrill of sitting in a meadow, of standing on a hillside, of enjoying the fragrance of wild flowers on a spring day, of lying in a basket listening to the songs of the meadow lark, of crawling in the sand, of hiding in the grass with a dog, or of sharing thoughts with a spotted fawn.

The sons and daughters of Tom Mitchell appeared so frequently in the Hudson canvases that it might have been appropriate to title the collection "The Mitchell Family Album." Tom and Clara's firstborn child, Taylor, or Tullo, had first appeared in pigment in 1897. He was followed in 1897, by their daughter Annie and in 1904 by Warfield.

Tom Mitchell, like Captain John Mewhinney many years earlier, divorced Clara in the speedy way of his people. He took a second wife, Mary Luff. The birth of a

67

fourth child by that union, Garland, occurred within two weeks. In time, Grace Hudson painted four portraits of Garland. To the last of these, she wrote a short commentary about her latest Mitchell subject:

Warfield is a sad little boy. He is an unwanted guest in the home of his stepfather and his stepgrandmother. His days are spent fishing or hunting for rabbits, squirrels or quail, in the effort to secure a welcome at night. The welcome, at best, is but the scraps from the dinner, which often he has provided. A little blanket on the floor is his bed for the night. He sometimes runs away to an uncle, but his love for his young mother, and knowing she will weep always, takes him back in a few days.

As usual, Grace had her father photograph each painting as it left her studio. One of the portraits, number "316," further illustrated that Grace sometimes changed her mind about a "finished" painting, as she had already shown with *The Orphan*. The unsigned, initial version of her portrait of Warfield was later changed by painting its rail fence background.

One of the most attractive of her paintings for the year was named *The Mystic Symbol*, number "309." The work was one of Grace's larger canvases, 30- by 31½-inches, and its two subjects were Mary Mitchell and Pete McClure. Pete was pictured as taking a break from wampum making to smoke his pipe, while Mary inspected the handiwork of a small Pomo basket.

Wampum money-making was a nearly full-time occupation for the Pomo men, as was basket making for the women. Collecting shells for the production of money required several trips each year more than fifty miles over wooded mountains to the Pacific Coast. The region near Bodega Bay was much favored by the Indians as a source of mollusks.

Even though no metal was used in the Pomo money, they called this form of their wampum *ka-yah*, or Indian silver. The shells were first broken into roughly-rounded disks, by hand with a stone, then smoothed with a quartz implement. Finally, a *ka-win*, or boring machine like the one pictured in *The Mystic Symbol* completed the bead. Often, hundreds of these patiently-produced coins were strung into long strands that were worn as a measure of stature and rank.

As had become more and more common, Grace wrote a brief commentary about *The Mystic Symbol* which explained something of the tradition of basketry among the Pomo:

Warfield Mitchell
Location Unknown

The Quail Woman who taught the Indians basketry bade them use certain symbols for her. She might come at any time and go from top to bottom of the basket and inspect the perfection of the work. The old folks tell the legend over and over to the young, urging them not to forget or neglect the principles of the beautiful Quail Woman and their ancestors. All designs on a Pomo basket have an opening in the design to allow the Quail Woman to enter the basket and inspect its quality.

By the close of the year, Grace Hudson had completed 25 new paintings.

. . . . .

Since late in 1907, Bruner's Gallery in Santa Rosa had been handling the Hudson collection. Whether it was the inconvenience of packing and shipping canvases, or the arduous trips to San Francisco that influenced Grace to find a market nearer to her Ukiah home, is impossible to tell. In the years between 1908 and 1912, her popularity swept Sonoma County, and within a short time the walls at Bruner's were covered with Grace's paintings.

To summarize the various painting of these years of the artist's career, a few picked at random may serve to indicate Grace Hudson's preferred subjects.

The Hunters, number "325," featured Grace's little misnamed friend, Tullo. The boy was 11 years old in 1908, and he seemed quite at ease posing for a portrait with his catch of the day. Several similar paintings, based upon either hunting or fishing scenes, dominate Grace's output early in the century. Included in this painting is Tullo's shaggy friend, who, without doubt, deserved much of the credit for the day's bag of two squirrels.

Grace's most ambitious work of 1908, and one of the largest paintings of her career, was of Rosa with Rekis in her arms. Numbered "330," it was titled variously *Chuly* and *The Little One*. Pomo women, especially younger ones, were indulgent with their small children, for their regular work was accomplished only when the children slept. If the mother was very young, as was oftentimes the case, her own mother, or another older female relative, would care for the baby while the mother worked.

Liberties taken by a gallery or a framer during later years has reduced *The Little One* from its original dimensions, 30- by 36-inches, as was recorded in Grace Hudson's painting diary, to 28½- by 30½-inches. This decision has not enhanced the perspective of the canvas, but perhaps was necessary because of damage to the painting's surface on one or more of its edges.

The Buffalo Maid, number "355," portrays a legendary siren of the Pawnee, not Pomo, tribe. More and more, Grace had become interested in the ethnological studies of her husband. The legendary maid was sent to lure away one of the Pawnee tribe who had offended the gods, but did not belong to a single Plains tribe. Grace painted the young woman wearing the costume of a midwestern tribe, carrying a vase from the Pueblos, and wearing her hair according to the tradition of the Pawnees.

The legend, as Dr. Hudson recorded, relates that the Buffalo Maid would lure her victim to a designated spot, then turn into a buffalo and mix with the herd. The unfortunate warrier would be left to wander forever, hoping to catch sight of his native tribe.

In the background of *The Buffalo Maid*, Grace painted Eagle Chief, considered by Dr. Hudson and his colleagues at the Field Museum to have been the most handsome Indian in North America.

Mity Warrier, number "360," which was painted in 1910, shows Warfield Mitchell out on a morning walk. Throughout their childhood, Pomos were told many stories, which they, in turn, passed on to their own children. One of the first legends was "How the Birds Got their colors."

The tale relates that, in the beginning, all birds of the sky were white. A long time ago, Gillock, a ghoul, stole the wife of Ta-ta, the hawk. This so disturbed all of the other birds that they decided to make war on Gillock. After carefully making the necessary plans for attack, they donned warpaint. The beautiful colors pleased them so much that they decided never to remove them.

Instead of joining the other birds, Tsy, the bluejay, decided he would keep watch for Gillock, on top of his lodge. So Tsy stood guard by the smoke hole and gave warning as the other feathered warriors approached. For Tsy's treachery, the blue jay was made to wear always the smoky blue color it bears today, and it became the most despised of birds, by birds and man alike. For this reason, it is Tsy who gives first warning when an invader approaches the sanctuary of the forest, and it is Tsy whom little Warfield hopes to shoot with his first arrow.

Grace completed several paintings on the theme of wildflowers during the years

A Buffalo Maid
Private Collection

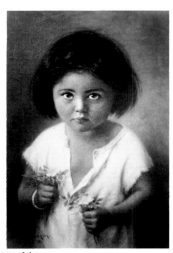

Wild Roses
Private Collection

between 1908 and 1912. Among them were *The First Lesson*, number "415," and *Kal-si* the *Wayside Flowers*, number "500." Like all children, the Pomo youngsters enjoyed walking through the fields of wildflowers in springtime, picking the golden blooms of the California poppy, columbine, trillium, lily of the valley, and others. *Ba-ka-kai*, number "506," was a typical youngster. Each of the young girls selected one particular flower which she could consider her own. The flower became, for them, a substitute for the feathers usually worn as finery by their elders in the ceremonial dances.

In a parallel theme, Grace depicted the young Pomo boys enjoying playful wild creatures. The aboriginal Indian was so close to nature that it was easy for him to believe that his ancestors once had been birds and animals. Each child was raised on legends about his heritage, and he became familiar with the history and personal traits of each wild creature, calling them his "little brothers." Paintings "367" and "417," give the feeling of having been, practically speaking, completed just minutes apart, not the more than two years that actually separate them. The choice of touching or being touched appeared to be endless for, in these canvases, the eye is endlessly drawn back and forth.

. . . . .

In 1910, Grace was entering a time for pausing and contemplating. She was now 45 years of age and wanted the security of permanent roots. The Hudson's dream, over the preceding years, had been of having a home especially designed for them. This dream was now moving towards realization.

Because of their respective interests, the house demanded the most up-to-date art studio which any painter and architect together could design. It required an equally-intriguing study, for John's anthropological activities necessitated many shelves of books and an expanse of desks. In addition, the total plan must have included many spaces for displaying the large collection of Hudson artifacts.

John and Grace hoped, additionally, that their future home would be something truly different, unique, and characteristic of its two uncommon residents.

With plans for the new house finally underway, Grace's production of new canvases focused on smaller, less intricate paintings. Of the 20 that she completed in 1910, only three were larger than 12 inches, and details of garments, still-life articles, and background were only suggested, instead of fully completed, as was more typically the case in her art.

Dr. Hudson, meanwhile, found himself faced by the overwhelming task of providing financing for their new home. He decided to seek a permanent home for his basket collection with a major museum. For a time, in 1910, the collection resided at the Park Museum, and it appeared that the efforts of more than 15 years of collecting would find a place to settle in that institution. In January, the Ukiah *Republican Press* reported:

The Hudson collection of Indian baskets, which was offered to the Park Commissioners as a loan a month ago, was formally accepted last week and is being installed at the Park Museum.

The commissioners are generally opposed to accepting any loans of this sort, but the value and interest of this collection caused them to make an exception. There is a clause in the acceptance which provides that the loan cannot be recalled under a year.

The new accession consists of the entire collection of Dr. J. W. Hudson of Ukiah, considered among the five best in the state. There are 194 examples of the best Pomo baskets and represent the gems of the collection. The most valuable *single piece is an oblong receptacle for trinkets, perhaps seven inches in length and three across. It is in a remarkably fine fabric—sixty-five stitches to the running inch—and has a beautiful wavy pattern in black and white. An offer of $240 was refused for this piece a short time ago. Perhaps the next-best specimen is a brown and white basket with a triangular pattern and as big as a washtub, but of close and firm textures.*

The remainder of the collection comprises samples of the work of every tribe on the Pacific Coast and baskets for every sort of use. There are water jugs, fishing baskets, receptacles for boiling and eating soup, papoose carriers and acorn bins of all shapes and sizes. Some of the most valuable in this section come from the Alaskan tribes. The finished baskets are all installed in two large cases and another section of the collection, illustrating the process of weaving among the Pomos, will be put in place this week. Dr. Hudson has lent with the collection a complete set of articles of ordinary use among the Pomos, including the vestments and instruments of their sacrificial dances.

Several months later, however, a newsclipping saved by Grace from a Washington, D. C. newspaper revealed:

The National Museum, through the Bureau of Ethnology, has just received from California the entire Hudson collection of Indian basketwork. This is the finest collection in existence. The museum collection now is not only the finest in the world, but one which never can be duplicated, as basketmaking is already a dying art among the Indians. The Hudson collection numbers about 250 pieces, at least half of which would be worth from $100.00 to $250.00 each in the market. It was made by Dr. J. W. Hudson during twenty-five years of intimate association with the Pomos and other Pacific Coast tribes. Many of the specimens are sacrificial baskets, which require from one to three years to make and are seldom secured by collectors, being burned on the death of their owners. The British Museum has been after this collection, but failed to secure it; Professor McGee, of the bureau, obtaining an option on it last year. The price to the National Museum was almost nominal.

For himself, John Hudson kept just a few of the finest Pomo baskets, planning storage and display areas into the new home. The structure, named by its new occupants, the "Sun House," was finally completed in 1912. Grace and John gratefully moved their belongings to the spacious home from their crowded previous dwelling. In the confusion of the move, nearly 15 paintings were sent to Bruner's Gallery in Santa Rosa without being photographed, and Grace omitted from her records the usual year heading found at the top of each page of her notebook.

For the first time in their married life, Dr. and Mrs. Hudson were settled in a home suitable to both of their vocations.

CHAPTER 7

THE LATER YEARS

Life in the Sun House

UNQUESTIONABLY the "Sun House" was the most dramatic and functional home in the area. From the massive redwood pillars of the front porch to the beamed ceilings of the bedrooms, it was truly remarkable. A special studio room for Grace was equipped with numerous windows and had its own fireplace to ensure comfort when she painted on winter days. Settled into this new environment, Grace turned to her easel with renewed energy and enthusiasm.

Of the twenty-three paintings completed in 1912, all were larger than ten inches. Her happiness and contentment reflected itself in her work. Previous accomplishments were merely stepping stones and, for her life was especially full.

One of the interesting characters of the Pomo culture was *Bu-ta Mad-tha, The Bear Woman*, number "406." Grace had not previously attempted to portray this mythical figure; with her new perspective, this was an appropriate time for such an undertaking. The Bear Woman was the secret judicial official of the Pomo community, whose duty was the punishment of those who broke the strict societal codes of the tribe. The office and all its accoutrements were hereditary. In some instances, the duties became the responsibility of a woman. The performance of the Bear Woman role demanded cunning, strength and agility, for failure to carry out the prescribed duties could mean disgrace and death. Her identity was known only to the village chief, who served as a patriarchal judge. The Bear Woman's paraphernalia consisted of a tanned bearskin sitted closely over the body, with the snout drawn forward over the wearer's forehead. The wearer's face was covered with a wicker mask and his or her body was encircled with hardwood rods to make it impenetrable to arrows and daggers. Hands and feet were left uncovered to assure freedom of movement.

Bear Woman
Private Collection

Thieves, pilferers, bullies, abusers of the weak and unfortunate, or any other offenders were given four warnings by the village chief; if these were disregarded, the offender became the target of Bu-ta Mad-tha. In planning an assault, the Bear Woman would study the trail habits used by the offender beyond the village. At the precise time when he was found alone and unaware, she would rush upon him with a roar and brandish her claws. Most victims would fall prone in terror, as Indians were especially afraid of bears. If his offense was grave, the offender was quickly dispatched by a deep stab above the collar bone. For less grievous crimes, the victim was deeply scored with an elk horn, as if mauled by the claws of a bear.

Among Grace Hudson's other notable studies of maturity are the paintings of an old hereditary chief of the Pomos, whom she portrayed several times. This

73

Kay-Will
Shasta State Historical Society

man, Kay-will, was a truly remarkable individual and lived a long and eventful life. When the Spanish established an outpost north of San Francisco Bay in 1835, little Kay-will was kidnapped, taken to the settlement, and sold as a slave. He was in the service of General Vallejo until he became a young man. The general taught him Spanish, his prayers, and some of the ways of hispanic society.

In 1847 Kay-will went to Lake County with the Stone and Kelsey expedition, where he quickly learned the native dialect and customs. The native population were so mistreated by Stone and Kelsey's expedition that one day, in an outrage, the Indians attacked the party. A bitter chapter was thus written in the history of the region. Pomo tradition holds the belief that it was Kay-will's knowledge of firearms that turned the massacre in favor of the Indians; he was responsible for loading the white men's weapons. Kay-will escaped and returned to his people, a free man. Upon the death of his brother, he became chief of the Shanel Pomos, near Hopland, south of Ukiah.

His natural sagacity, benign disposition, and knowledge of the white man's customs made Kay-will a popular leader. He formed close friendships with the arriving farmers, and when he saw his own people being crowded out of their home valley, he borrowed money and bought a tract of land for the settlement of his tribe. The Shenal Pomos picked hops until this debt was repaid.

Kay-will was the money broker of his tribe and made regular trips to Bodega Bay to secure the clam shells with which to make wampum. He hired skilled coiners to chip, bore and polish the shells. Kay-will was an orator, master of many Pomo dialects, and counselor and consoler to both young and old. Sometimes he would give advice at great length, or he would just sit in deep meditation.

Most notable of Grace's paintings of Kay-will were numbers "407" and "408," both titled *Portrait of a Pomo Chief.*

Portraits of infants and children far outnumbered those of adults. The reasons for this were probably many and varied. When Grace did find a cooperative and friendly adult, such as Joseppa, Kay-will, Mollie Duncan, Mary Pinto, or Eba, she painted them several times. Eba as *Do-Sho-Ya*, a matron, in canvas "373," appeared again in "404," making a basket, and in "406," as *The Bear Woman*. Four full-length portraits of the woman were completed between 1911 and 1913. Each of these, numbers "377," "395," "409," and "437," had similar backgrounds, still-life studies of Pomo baskets, and costumes.

Pomo dancing was a ceremony requiring elaborate costuming, and Eba was the model for the female dance attire in canvas "412," *The Wi-ly.* Grace wrote an interesting commentary on this work.

The time had arrived for the Wi-ly *to begin. A fire separated the large gathering of men, women and children on one side and the musicians and dancers on the other. While the audience is anxiously awaiting the appearance of the performers, we will take a look at their costumes while they are applying the finishing touches to their makeup.*

The men are wearing breech cloths of animal skins. On their backs, hanging from the shoulders, are overlapping feathers from the wings and tails of eagles and buzzards. These are arranged about the width and length of the body in such a manner that the feathers quiver and float in the air with every movement of the dance. Across the forehead is a band some six inches wide, woven in a manner that makes it appear to be a beautiful orange ribbon with black edges. This is made of the tail feathers of the yellow hammer. The ends of the feathers, which are black, are cut in diamond shapes and reversed in the pattern of weaving to produce the desired effect. This band extends about six inches, from directly over the ear, allowing the ends to flap with the movements of the head. Little tufts of eagle down, applied with pitch, are dotted all over the body. Black and red markings decorate the face in straight and saw-tooth lines.

Full-length, highly polished leg bones of the eagle are worn in the lobes of the ears. Sticks, a foot or more in length, decorated at one end with tufts and fancy gigs of feathers, are carried in the hands. This completes the costume.

The women wear a kow-ty. *This is a dark-brown dirndle-like skirt fastened about the waist, and reaches well to the knees. It is made from the inner bark of a special variety of large willow. In its preparation there is a hand treatment which renders it soft and pliable. Across the forehead is a band of mink or otter skin, from which quills support pendants and bangles. A huge top-knot of feathers completes the headdress. Quantities of wampum adorn the neck and arms. This completes the costume, except for some feathers carried in the hand.*

The musicians come and are seated on the ground, well back of the fire. Their instruments are split quills, wooden whistles, clapping sticks, etc. There is no disagreeable scraping and tuning up or mending of broken strings. The orchestra begins at once and the dancers come on single file, in a turkey trot.

The women take their places in front of the musicians. The men follow, circling about and occupying the area closer to the fire. There is no rushing or crowding for places.

A Dancer
Private Collection

The number to dance depends upon the feathers that are available. None are to dance except those properly costumed. Sometimes there are no more than three, but, on great occasions, as many as twelve men may dance at one time. The number of men and women dancers is not consistent.

For the women there is comparatively little movement of the body. The steps are very slight and confined to a mere spot of ground. The forearms are extended, holding the hands about two feet apart; without changing the relative distance, they are carried from side to side.

The men prance and stamp and circle about, crouching in a mimic warfare. Each dancer carries a whistle in his mouth. They drone a sing-song, inter-mingled with explosive grunt and blowing whistle. Each is independent of the other movements, yet all are in time to the rhythm of the music. The timing and rhythm vary with different dances.

The music and dance end suddenly, in a tremendous grunt, and the spectators give a prolonged "hi-e-e-e," as the dancers retire. There is no applause.

The Hudsons' great interest and profound empathy for the Pomo Indians opened many doors that might very well have been closed to any other white people. Many of the distorted stories or half-truths that were told to passing anthropologists for a meagre pay of fifty cents an hour were conjured up for the benefit of the moment. The Hudsons recorded many true stories and the descriptions often added a depth of meaning to paintings that otherwise might well be viewed as just another portrait.

Two delightful studies completed in 1912 were *Col-lip-win*, number "419" and *Mad-tha-koo*, number "420."

Willum was a wandering fisherboy with no place he could call home. He stayed wherever he could find shelter, with relatives, friends, or even with strangers, for his true home offered only a step-father and a step-grandmother, neither of whom liked boys very much. Willum sometimes wandered as far as 60 miles away from Ukiah, and he seldom attended school, worked, or obeyed anyone. He ate when he was hungry, drank when he was thirsty, and slept when he was tired.

During the long summer days, he played with his dog chasing young rabbits or catching squirrels. Willum would move the piles of hop poles, and his dog would attack the squirrels as they attempted to find another place of shelter. The rest of the time they fished and were happy companions. When they were tired, hungry,

75

or just needed a place to stay, they camped in the backyard of the Sun House with Grace and John Hudson. The rest of the time they lived in a brush hut on the banks of the Russian River.

The second painting of the pair was of the Pomo Indian girl named *Mad-tha-koo*. Grace wrote:

> Up until the time of puberty her life was as carefree and joyous as the birds of the air and the animals of the forest; however, the time had come when she must learn minor household duties. She is given a large shallow basket partially full of hulled acorns. With a stone pestle the acorns are ground into a meal and then leached in the river to remove irritants. It is then heated with hot rocks and prepared into a mush. The young lady has prepared her first dinner.

One of the finest painting of 1912, if not of the entire collection, was of a Pomo Medicine man, number "414." The story accompanying this painting was related to the artist's mother, Helen Carpenter, by her lifelong Indian friend, Captain John Mewhinney.

> When a Pomo Indian becomes ill it is necessary for two doctors to attend him. One will diagnose the ailment and the other will furnish the remedy. The first step in diagnosis is to gash the patient and suck some of his blood.
>
> Everything is supposed to be able to talk; a leaf, a bird, an animal, or a crooked stick . . . It is the duty of the doctor to determine which one has caused the illness. On occasion the patient will have a distinct recollection of an unbelievable creature. If an effigy can be constructed some hopes of recovery is imminent. The sight of the culprit may produce alarm and on occasion convulsions. The more alarming the response the greater the chance of recovery. The Medicine man's paraphernalia consists of charms, whistles, feathers, rattles, robes, etc. These are carefully guarded by the Medicine man to ensure his own safety.
>
> One evening at the Willy, Chapo became ill. The Medicine man was summoned to the sha where Chapo lay suffering from abdominal pain. Judging from his prolonged groaning and writhing movements it was time to call for assistance. Everything that could be thought of was displayed but to no avail. He got steadily worse. Four deep gashes in each temple and several on his arm brought no relief. Things appeared hopeless . . .
>
> The doctor broke and destroyed the beautiful head band of flicker feathers and the elaborate waist mantel. Then he danced on the broken pieces, singing and chanting as he performed many weird movements. The evil spirits departed.
>
> The Ma-tu was convinced that Chapo would either get well or die so he too departed. Chapo's wife cried and chanted all through the night as she kept her lonely vigil. As the pains subsided Chapo fell asleep.

. . . . .

Pomo Medicine Man
Private Collection

The years between 1913 and 1925 were among the artist's most important, for in these years she explored many subjects with a depth and patience even greater than shown in her earlier works. Indeed, this period easily could be referred to as her remarkable fifties. Throughout the decade which formed the bulk of this portion of her life, her work was impeccable, unparalled at any other time in her career. No portrait left Grace's easel until every minute detail had been refined and honed until it pleased her critical eye. She had long been considered a good painter by her friends and patrons; now she began to focus her attention on becoming a great painter.

76

In 1913, for the first time since she had recorded her paintings, she began to identify the month in which each was completed. The days of the small, 5-by 7-inch or even 10- by 14-inch canvases seemingly were over, and many paintings as large as 30 inches were produced.

Like other creative artists, Grace Hudson often took liberties that left the researcher or historian baffled. A case in point was that of her painting of Annie Mitchell, *Ud-dool, The Only One*, number "426."

Annie was painted in 1913 by Grace as she appeared at the approximate age of 18 months. One studying Hudson's career was aware that, in that year, Annie was actually 13 years of age. Did Grace paint this picture from memory or complete an unfinished canvas started 12 years before? Did she come across an old sketch which appealed to her and decide that it would provide a good subject for a canvas? These questions will never be answered, of course, but by considering them the true nature of her talent may be better revealed.

Although Grace Hudson kept records of her paintings throughout her life in far greater detail than most artists, it was not unusual for her portraits to be recorded without listing the specific identity of the sitter. Such paintings as *Pomo Indian Baby with Apple*, number "434;" *Indian Child with Fawn*, number "439;" *Pomo Indian Children in Ma-tu Woods*, number "440;" and *Pomo Child with Dog*, number "442" provide a few examples of anonymous subjects.

Hu-hi-ya and Bu-shay
Private Collection

One such canvas, *The Talking Fawn*, another title for number "439," illustrated another Pomo myth concerning the wife of Ta-ta, the hawk—who later was stolen by Gillock. Ta-ta's wife became angry with her spouse and prevented him from talking with his little son. Ta-ta would follow their tracks through the forest, but when he came close to them, the mother would turn herself into a doe and the son into a fawn. She once told her son, the fawn, to go deep into the dark woods and to wait there for her. Ta-ta, not recognizing his wife in her disguise, shot her with an arrow, killing her. The fawn wandered the forest, asking every deer he met, "Have you seen my mother?"

Grace's little subject believed her particular fawn to be the very one that was Ta-ta's son, and hoped that, if she followed him into the woods, she could hear him speak to the other deer.

A similar story was the subject of *Hu-hi-ya and Bu-shay*, number "525." The two subjects, human and deer, wandered through the woods, for the little girl had no brother, sister, dog, or doll, only the amusement and companionship of the wild-but-gentle creatures of the forest.

One day, she was sitting very still watching a squirrel, when tiny Bu-shay walked straight to her and said, "Take me home! Take me home!" At least so Hu-hi-ya told her mother when she reached home with Bu-shay in her arms. The deer took easily to pinole, Hu-hi-ya's bed, and Indian ways, but no one except Hu-hi-ya ever heard him speak.

To detail all the paintings worthy of mention during this productive part of Grace Hudson's life would require many pages, for virtually every canvas produced between 1913 and 1925 was, in some way, remarkable. One of the most amazing aspects of Grace's entire life story was her ability to maintain consistent quality and technique during her career, despite many events which might have distracted a less-purposeful artist. Influenza, a sprained ankle, major surgery, even the death in two years of both of her parents cannot be shown to have affected the paintings she produced, for if Grace Hudson felt she could not apply herself to her art with the dedication, concern, and awareness that characterized all of her work, she merely put down her brushes for a time.

To characterize her production, the more than 190 paintings which left her easel during this period may be separated into just a few categories. As was her style earlier in her career, she continued to concentrate her effort on recording portraits of Indian infants and children, illustrating legends and traditions, painting the faces of the elderly, and illuminating the workings of the Native American mind.

One looking at her canvases for the first time might feel that a great similarity existed between many of her paintings. It is only the unobservant viewer, however, who retains this feeling after a longer exposure to her work.

While skin color, eye formation, hair color, and other anatomical landmarks were similar within the Pomo race, each individual was unique. This became especially noticeable in the various portraits which Grace Hudson painted. Each subject, in his or her simple costume, may be seen to resemble in pose, yet never duplicate in appearance, any other figure in any other canvas.

As was the case earlier in her life, some of her paintings drew comments in the press. *He Loves You*, number "451," was completed during 1914 and was shipped to Gump's in San Francisco. The following article, prompted by the painting, appeared in the June 21, 1914 issue of the *San Francisco Chronicle*:

Of the innumerably interesting pictures shown to the public by Grace Hudson, probably no one surpasses a canvas which is to be seen in the Gump's Galleries. Though it has been stated often that Mrs. Hudson in her mountain home in Mendocino County is deeply familiar with Indian life and lore, through a close contact seldom allowed to white people, it is still impressive that she has been able to gain so much of the intimacy of legendry, especially as much of it borders upon the sacred.

In this new canvas, the Song of the Lark [as the gallery renamed it], *Mrs. Hudson has drawn right from life, pictured literally a poetic story. According to the precepts of the Indians, no Indian maid must ever listen to the singing of the lark, even though its message is the sweetest of all to the girl's ear. It is not the harbinger of sorrow nor trouble in any sense, but the innate instinct (grounded for centuries) of the Indian mother to protect her daughter from the power of love. The lark sings of love, and, when his voice is lifted in spring, a dutiful Indian girl turns away, though sadly.*

Grace Hudson wrote many commentaries about her subjects, some of which have already been quoted or paraphrased. These accompanied the paintings to the art dealers. Many explanations attached to the early paintings were discarded or lost, but copies of the commentaries to paintings purchased during her later years were kept at the Sun House. One described *The Lonesome Hour*, number "452."

The hours between sunset and dark, when the birds are hushed, every creature thinks of home.

The Mai-du *bride will always be an alien among the Pomos. Her Pomo husband is usually her only companion, but occasionally a friend from her own people will come to visit. When the women go out to work, she works alone—using her own* Mai-du *basket. The women in the background are leeching acorn meal. They dig a hole in the sand, pat it hard inside, put the meal in and place the open basket over it. Water is then poured through it until the bitter taste is removed. When the meal is dry, it can be removed in cakes clean and free from sand. The background is a bit of the Russian River near Ukiah.*

The fields and streams of Mendocino County, in 1915, were still abundant with wildlife. Men of the diminished tribe of Pomo could still hunt and catch deer, and young boys could try their luck on smaller animals with a bow and arrow. They often were successful and brought home rabbits or gray squirrels for the family dinner.

Natives, number "462," revealed a young marksman with his bounty. His small game bow was made of willow with a sinew string. The arrow was a single shaft of willow with only a sharpened point.

Everyday events such as food gathering commanded care and thought from Grace Hudson as she prepared each canvas on the subject. If such commonplace activities were important to her, however, she focused even more carefully, when her subject was a Pomo legend. The Pomos, like all Indians, remained very superstitious despite their contact with the whites.

One myth, regarding the rain, was the subject of several Hudson paintings—numbers "461," "484," "517," and "524." Each showed little children in the middle of nowhere, protected only by a tattered umbrella. *The Adventurers*, number "524" and the last of the series, was accompanied by Grace's complete explanation of the theme.

Natives
Private Collection

Gimini was so filled with pride in the possession of the missionary's old umbrella that he persuaded his sister into a runaway expedition to see it work. They took the trail to grandma's camp. Unfortunately, their progress was delayed by a tired baby sister and the rain began to fall rather heavily. Gimini remembered how folks had been swooped up to the sky by the entangling skirts of Ma-ki-la Mad-tha *the Rain Woman. They were having misgivings about the adventure.*

The black cloud that gathers in the west before a storm is Ma-ki-la *the Thunder Man. The thunder is* Ma-ki-la's *call for* Ma-ki-la Mad-tha, *the Rain Woman. The Rain Woman rised up from the eastern mountains, casting lightning glances in search of* Ma-ki-la. *As she crosses the sky and meets him, the rain shakes from her garments in long, fringe-like strings, with a soft rustling sound. After she returns to her home in the east, the rain ceases and the sun comes out.*

The old Indians are cautious about being abroad during a thunderstorm, believing that the entangling skirts of Ma-ki-la Mad-tha *might snatch them up into the sky.*

The Adventurers
Private Collection

Pomo mythology cast the brown owl as the bogey man. *Ma-ku-ku* is apt to be about anytime after sunset and watches for naughty children, especially those who have been crying or fussing. The small girl seen in *We Got Him*, canvas "466," evidently insisted on staying at the house with her little brother; but it became late, and darkness rapidly approached. Possibly it is *Ma-ku-ku* that made the strange noises which held their apprehensive attention.

The background of *We Got Him* is the entrance and interior of a Pomo summer dwelling, probably located near the hop fields. These huts were cleverly woven with both living and cut brush and tied together with wild grape-vine fibers. Inside the hut, Grace painted a big basket used to store acorns, and a mortar basket without a bottom.

One of the most popular models of all those Grace Hudson painted was Culin Mitchell. Culin had been born on December 25, 1910, the eighth child of Tom Mitchell. She never lacked for care, attention, or playmates. All of the Mitchell children were, of course, portrayed by Grace Hudson, but Culin seems to have caught the special attention of the "painter lady," for over 20 Hudson portraits were identified by the artist as being of the youngster. She posed with apples, butterflies, rabbits, chipmunks, squirrels, foxes, and her brothers and sisters.

Although Culin's first portrait, number "396," was completed in the latter part of 1911, it was not until September, 1915 that she appeared again on canvas. Grace wrote of the portrait, number "471," that Culin was a little Pomo girl who wished she were white. Tom Mitchell was employed on a Ukiah valley farm, and,

whenever possible, his tiny daughter would slip away from the family cabin and
follow her father to the farm house, where she would shyly watch the farmer's
wife. She often would not depart until almost dark, and then only at the suggestion of the person of her fascination. When summer came, the Mitchell family
often camped in the pasture back of the Sun House. Once, while she was there,
Culin saw a little white girl of her own age, wearing a very short dress. Culin was
attired at the time in a rather long gingham shirt with two red bows in her hair.
Suddenly, its hemline was no longer to her liking and she explored Grace's studio
until she found a pair of scissors and shortened her garment in conformity
with the latest *ma-san* style. Quite heedless of any wishes of her father, mother
and five brothers, she also felt her hair was longer than the current fashion, and
re-styled her tresses. Her new look was apparently attractive, for Culin seemed
quite pleased with herself. She evidently gave up trying to look like little *ma-san*
girls in short dresses, however, because each successive portrait by Grace depicted
her in a long dress.

While Culin was an infant, a friend brought her some madrone berries. She
developed such a fondness for the berries that her family began calling her *Chi-
bot-ta*, meaning "wild pigeon." This was Grace Hudson's title in 1915 for canvas
number "475," a portrait of four-year old Culin. *Chi-bot-ta's* happy expression is
due to her enjoyment of the story, "The Three Bears," which Grace developed
and enlarged especially for her. Culin's constant request, as she posed for her
friend *Mad-tha-coo*, was "Tell little me hear say." If Grace's response was not
prompt, it became, "Mad-tha-coo, say hi." With "Hi," it was back to the beginning, "Mad-tha-coo tell little me hear say."

On August 1, 1915, Culin was joined by the latest addition to the Mitchell
family, a brother named Shaili. The boy appeared with Culin in two paintings,
numbered "493" and "538."

Culin Mitchell and Shaili
Private Collection

There was nothing too fine for a new male child, so the Mitchells took him to
town and had him christened in the white man's manner. When the priest asked
the baby's name, his mother replied, "Shaili." He asked again, and again she
repeated the name. The padre hesitated a moment, then baptized the child "John
Michael Francis Sebastian." The mother and children slipped away noiselessly
and, like frightened rabbits, hustled through the gate to the painter lady's house.
When the door was closed behind them, they all began at once to tell her about
the incident and asked, "Won't Shaili be Shaili anymore?" They were somewhat
reassured when she told them that the long *ma-san* name was to be placed in a big
book, and that Shaili would still be Shaili; however, they took no risks. Whenever
the priest visited the rancheria, the older boys carried Shaili into the woods. In
these two canvases, Culin watched over Shaili, while the boys stood guard to warn
of the priest's coming.

Culin had almost reached her ninth birthday when she posed in the forest with
her pet fox, received as a kit when the child had the measles. The painting, number "533," was originally titled *The Plotters*.

The domesticated fox soon was named Con-cu and became an established member of the Mitchell family, receiving the privileges and protections of the household. He played and slept with Culin, and she, in turn, adopted many of his wood-
sy habits. On warm Autumn days, when she should have been in the Mission
School with the other Pomo children, Culin frolicked in the woods with Con-cu,
climbing trees, hunting mice, eating berries or just sporting in the leaves. Their
popularity around the camp left a great deal to be desired. When drying meat, fish
or fruit were scattered or missing, or any other light mischief done in the rancheria, the injured party usually accused the two foxes, Culin and her pet. *The
Foxes* was the name chosen to retitle Grace's portrayal of this pair, the painting

which appears as the cover illustration of this book.

Grace's final portrait of Culin, *The Hop Picker*, number "575," was painted in 1923, when the Indian girl was twelve years old.

. . . . .

Few events in the lives of Grace and John Hudson could slow the flow of canvases from the Sun House in Ukiah, but in February, 1917, the death of the artist's mother, Helen McCowen Carpenter, caused Grace to lay her brushes aside.

Helen Carpenter had become increasingly frail with the passing years, but the Mendocino County pioneer had remained dear to many people in Ukiah and Potter Valley. An eulogy by Jenny Sturtevant MacMillan, which appeared in the Ukiah *Republican Press* on March 23, eloquently conveyed the love and respect family and friends had held for Helen:

> *This learned I from the shadow of a tree,*
> *That to and fro did sway upon a wall:*
> *Our shadow selves, our influence may fall*
> *Where we can never be.*

And while my life lasts, Mrs. Helen McCowen Carpenter, I shall feel the influence of your justice, thoughtfulness, kindness and love. . . .

Yours was ever an attitude of wholesome, unwavering justice, and so the play day closed in sweet memories of you.

We all laughed when I went to visit Grace to get the measles so I might be done with the "measly things." We laughed until the laugh almost ceased within me. . . .

So the years went, and was there ever a mother kinder or more patient to girls as they grew into womanhood than you were? Never one. My parents were so busy on ranch or farm that you helped the two of us dress when I was so frequently your guest. Your faithful daughter, May, was married and gone by this time.

The Hop Picker (Culin)
Private Collection

Grace and I had most of the upstairs and nearly all else to ourselves. A kindly hostess you always remained, even if we ran all day, danced half the night, for butterflies we surely were. Your greeting was always a smile of patience and affection. You had a warm bath in readiness for us and a delightful repast. How determined you were that we should laugh long and be as merry as possible! No look or act of yours ever reminded us of life being serious How well you knew that all too soon the lessons would be taught to us as to all! . . .

In later years you were the sympathetic friend or the joyous one, according to our experiences. Even our final meetings were a happy mixture of childhood days, when we gathered in your backyard or gathered about you for a story. At our last visiting, you bound up my bleeding foot, pierced by a nail, and read to us about your girlhood adventure of "crossing the plains". . . .

Ka-wi-lote
Private Collection

Grace completed only eleven canvases during 1917, all finished during the first nine months of the year. She did not pick up her brushes again until March of 1918.

The five-hundred series of Hudson paintings, begun just after her mother's death in 1917, spanned a period of almost ten years and represented some of the finest canvases in the entire Hudson *oeuvre*. *Ka-wi-lote*, "501," portrayed a newborn, unnamed infant. The Pomos called all newborns *ka-wi-lote* and the child of Grace's canvas never was properly named, for his mother departed without him for Chicago before either finishing his transport basket or deciding on a name. Weeks

81

and months passed and the infant's mother did not return. He was destined to be called *Ka-wi-lote*, the unnamed, all his life.

Annoyed and embarrassed, relatives took him to Mrs. Carpenter for her assistance in dealing with the nameless, abandoned infant. Rising to the occasion, Helen rummaged in her attic and produced a grand baby carriage. Though still just *Ka-wi-lote*, the problem of a carrying basket had been solved rather ingeniously, and he was trundled home like the finest *ma-san* child.

Many Pomo children's names reflected the influence of the Catholic missionary schools in the territory, for young Indian mothers often attended mission services. Hol-di-wit gave her baby the two most beautiful names she had ever heard, Mary Angel, believing that they would connect the baby with the Church and ensure a good life for her. Every service day, little Mary Angel, in her *hi-ka-tole* or transport basket, would sit by her mother on the foremost pew. If Mary Angel would get tired and begin to fuss, her mother would quietly rock the *hi-ka-tole* and the little basket swinging from the supporting hoop would amuse the infant. In Hol-di-wit's spiritual ambition, she did not fail to attend to the practical. The little basket was not only for Mary Angel's amusement, but intended as a charm to assure her talents as a fine weaver, synonymous among the Pomos as being a good housewife and mother. For Grace, the child became another beautiful canvas, *Mary Angel*, number "504."

While the rest of the world was occupied with World War I, Grace Hudson continued to paint, though not as prolifically as before.

Art frequently tends to be set aside during periods of crisis, but on February 16, 1918, the ladies of the Saturday Afternoon Club in Santa Rosa, California, decided to forget about the war for a time and turn to the arts for a little pleasant relaxation. Members loaned their Grace Hudson paintings and their Pomo basket collections for the enjoyment of all. Mrs. Frederick King had obtained an article on Grace Hudson, written by the artist's aunt, Mrs. Hale McCowen. It became the focal point of the club program.

Grace Hudson always had the disposition to do beyond her years and the ability to form whatever her fancy might dictate. When but four years of age, she was an artist in designing doll's wardrobes. She manufactured completely, not only for her own dolls, but for those of girls much older than herself, from patterns of her own design and cutting.

During her art-school days in San Francisco, she was acclaimed for her draftsmanship with a gold medal. In the life-model classes, she was termed the "lightning striker," because of the rapidity with which she worked.

Mrs. Hudson's method of procedure in working out an idea is, no doubt, similar to those used by other noted artists. When she has an inspiration, she first considers the Indians at her disposal to model. She selects the one in whose face she finds the expression best calculated to bring forth her idea. She then selects a sketch which she has made during an outing or vacation. Using this as a background, she works out her inspiration, to portray some feature of the Indian culture.

Her beautiful new bungalow-style home is located on Main Street in Ukiah. The studio is a large, airy, well-lighted room, which is most admirably adapted for the purpose it was intended. A visit to this home is a pleasure long to be remembered. The floors are polished oak and every nook and corner is filled with rare curios, antiques, rare, old hand-carved furniture and souvenirs from every part of the world. Although usually well adapted to entertaining, only once has Mrs. Hudson thrown her home open to the public. This was upon the occasion of a Belgian tea. Many people availed themselves of the opportunity to obtain a view of such art treasures that are seldom seen in such an isolated section of the country.

Mrs. Hudson is most hospitably inclined, but she has won for herself the name of being somewhat inhospitable and unsociable. She cannot allow visitors at any and all hours, due to the concentration and intensity with which she paints. Therefore, she maintains certain rules in regard to company, which some people find difficult to understand.

There are many amusing incidents in connection with Mrs Hudson's visitors. A visitor once commented, "I suppose these paintings are ordered by the children's parents." To us who know the Indians so well and are familiar with their lives of poverty, we might feel such a remark amusing. We could not help but wonder if the Indians' homes in other parts of the country are decorated with expensive oil portraits.

Grace's flow of paintings slowed again in 1919, when her father died. By this time, there were few of the early pioneers of Mendocino County still living, and A. O. Carpenter had been one of its major figures. The Ukiah newspaper of February 14, 1919, carried as its headline, "Pioneer of Journalism is Summoned." The story went on to report:

As one who wraps the drapery of his couch about him and lies down to pleasant dreams, A. O. Carpenter, pioneer rancher, politician and journalist, passed peacefully into the great beyond at an early hour last Saturday morning. The funeral was held from the residence last Sunday p.m., the service being conducted at graveside by the Odd Fellows Lodge, of which the deceased has been a lifelong member.

Grace had placed the finishing touches on *A Little Savage*, number "522," early on the day in which the article appeared; it was not until April of 1919 that she again took her paintbrushes in hand. Perhaps done in remembrance of her father, *Pinole for the Dead*, number "527," was her first effort.

Indians shuddered at the thought of the grave—of burying the soul. Just as it was a Pomo belief that the soul of the deceased was set free and purified by flames, they also believed that it was necessary to nourish the spirit of the departed for a year. This privilege fell to the nearest relative, or chief mourner, who took pinole in a basket to a place hallowed by the memory of the dead. The pinole was scattered over the ground at dawn.

For the remainder of 1919 and the early spring of 1920, Grace Hudson returned her attention to the young children of the Pomo, whom she depicted happily pursuing the joys of life. Among her subjects were many of her friends: Greenie, Hudson Mitchell, and others. In a few canvases, she painted the older Pomos: John Scott and Eva. Then, her work again ceased.

. . . . .

"You will never be able to work again."

The pronouncement came as a shock. Grace had not been in good health during the winter of 1919-1920, but she had never feared that it would be as bad as her doctor now indicated. Fortunately, Grace was able to prove the prediction false. She journeyed to San Francisco with her husband, where her physical problem was diagnosed as a thyroid condition. Surgery was prescribed, but Dr. Hudson and Grace hesitated.

The procedure was related in complete detail to John Hudson, and he was invited to gown for a similar operation to observe the proposed surgery. Although he had not practiced his profession for more than 20 years, he agreed to watch the procedure. To his dismay, and to that of the attending physician, the patient succumbed on the operating table, victim of a "thyroid storm." More than ever, the couple felt such a treatment would be unwise.

Instead, radium tubes were implanted in the artist's neck to retard the developing goiter; they remained there for the final 17 years of her life. The small red marks produced on the skin from the radiation sources deep within her neck prompted Grace to wear a wardrobe with high necklines for the rest of her life.

In time a heart condition also developed that at first was assumed to be the result of Grace's toxic thyroid condition; it was treated with digitalis. A considerable weight loss stopped the treatment as Dr. Hudson once again intervened. He reported that his wife had never had a normal heartbeat in her life and the medication was discontinued. Grace Hudson returned from San Francisco to Ukiah "skinny as a rail." With several months' rest and a hearty diet, however, she slowly began to add weight to her emaciated frame. Her recovery was slow and left her exhausted after any attempt to paint. As she gained strength, however, she could not avoid the temptation of returning to the activity that she loved most.

Rumors occasionally circulated in the art world that Dr. Hudson was really the Ukiah painter of the Pomos, not Grace, or that he signed all the paintings. These beliefs were fantasy, nothing more. The doctor was a student of Indian culture, and, to be sure, a respected authority in the field. What was quite probable was that he assisted Grace in writing some of the "salesman's notes" that accompanied her paintings.

The fifth canvas completed in 1920, *Culin and Shaili*, number "538," was accompanied by just such a note:

Since the high cost of living after the war, the painter lectured the Indians, collectively, individually, in small groups and on every occasion possible on the benefits of their own natural foods. She stressed the importance of gathering and storing supplies for the winter, just as their ancestors had done. She urged them to gather acorns, buckeyes and tubers, in the valleys and to go to Clear Lake and the coast for fish—to get corn, wheat, potatoes and fruit from the farmers who gave generously to their laborers. She showed them her own cellar and emphasized the cost of ma-san commodities.

The results were better than she anticipated. During the winter many friends came by to tell her what they had stored. The leader of a party of thirteen families related what each family had brought home from the coast. They had three hop bales (a measurement with which they were readily familiar) of dried seaweed, three hop bales of dried surf fish, two gunny sacks of dried abalone, two gunny sacks of dried mussels and a sack of dried candle fish. They also had quantities of salted salmon and forty quarts of wild berries.

Some of the group hadsraised their own corn and potatoes, while others worked on ranches, taking part of their wages in produce.

Several members helped harvest the county's bountiful fruit crop. They canned or dried apples, pears and prunes that were not suitable for marketing. All of these were exchanged or shared with the group.

The elderly people did their part by leaching and drying the acorn meal. Thus, going back to their old ways and incorporating some new ideas, they were getting along better than ever.

Art patrons from 1914 to 1922 had carried Hudson canvases away from Gump's San Francisco store almost as soon as they were hung. By spring of the latter year, however, they experienced a disappointment. Two portraits, numbers "552," of Green Scott, and "553," of Kol-pa, were the final pictures to be sold before Grace's contract with Gump's expired on April 30, 1922. With the conclusion of the exclusive Gump's arrangement, the artist began selling canvases once again through Bruner's Fine Art Gallery in Santa Rosa. In June, Grace noted in her diary, "Junior Contract," opposite the entry for painting number "558." Several paintings were sold by a Mr. Junior; however, this contract must not have been satisfactory, for in less than a year Hudson canvases were again being offered for sale at Bruner's.

Even as Grace Hudson approached her sixtieth birthday, there was little cause for a viewer to make excuses for lack of perfection in her paintings. She was long-since the best known artist of Indian subjects, and one could only wonder what boundaries she might have reached had she not restricted her talent to such a limited field. The confinements of race, creed, or color seldom enter one's mind while looking at her paintings, however, for the beauty of a single moment captured forever in her oils prompts only admiration.

The year 1925 was a scant one for Hudson paintings; only nine were completed. Waning enthusiasm or failure of talent was not responsible; instead, the Hudsons decided at mid-year to return to Europe. Their first trip to the continent had evidently not been sufficient to satisfy their interest in the beauty of the old masters or the quality of European architecture. The fulfillment and fatigue felt at the end of their other visit had long since passed, and the Hudsons looked forward to their trip with eager anticipation.

Grace put aside her easel and packed her trunks, departing in June for six delightful months abroad. For a time, the rolling hills and colorful residents of Ukiah were put far from her and John Hudson's minds.

CHAPTER 8

THE FINAL YEARS

Completion of a Life Work

OF THE FORTY YEARS in which Grace Hudson actively pursued a career as an artist, the last ten were her least productive. As most people pass three score years in life, it is natural that the energy of youth wanes. Still, some excellent paintings emerged during this quiet time in her life—a few may be among the finest she ever accomplished.

Both she and John Hudson had returned from their recent trip to Europe ready to renew their respective endeavors. The first painting Grace completed in 1926 was a typical example of a canvas finished after she had been away from her work for a long time. The result of hours of planning, and including the most minute details, it was titled *Children with a Bird's Nest*, number "601."

Children with a Bird's Nest
Private Collection

Her work on the canvas was delayed for a time by a prolonged case of flu. During the later years of her life, illness occasionally kept Grace from painting, for the influenza epidemics that had swept the United States did not spare rural Ukiah. Young persons frequently recovered in a short time, but the illnesses were particularly serious for the elderly who were sometimes ill for a month or more. Grace wrote "Influenza" in her painting diary in January, 1926, and only two canvases besides *Children with a Bird's Nest* were completed by May of that year.

Her later years were also a time to explore many paths previously ignored. She hooked rugs, adorning the floors of the Sun House and, for the first time tried her hand at sculpture. Like any artist working in two dimensions, the lure of sculpture was difficult to ignore. Her most notable attempt was a small cast of a jack rabbit, among the most plentiful of animals found in the fields surrounding Ukiah. Her pose portrayed the creature standing in alarm, on its hind legs, ears straight above its head. The form was a sight familiar to the artist, as it would be to any young lad on his first hunting trip.

Grace's sculpture of the rabbit still may be seen by passersby at the Sun House, where it is most frequently on view on the banister of the home's porch, overlooking a garden. On occasion, it wanders to another location in the yard.

Grace also attempted five small figurines of an Indian infant, resembling her portrait of Culin in *Primatives*, painting number "614." A miniature fur cape was wrapped about the shoulders of the tiny figures in the manner dictated by Indian customs and traditions. These statues have remained either among the family of the artist or with her close friends. None, however, were as successful as her oils.

Later life was also a time in which Grace Hudson could explore the few themes of Indian life that she previously had felt too illusive or complex. On only two

The Bride
Private Collection

occasions, for example, had she attempted to record the intricate beauty of the Pomo Indian betrothal ornamentation. These were paintings "158" and "212." Two new treatments on the subject of marriage were finished in 1927 and 1928, *The Betrothed*, number "612," and *Di-hi-da*, number "625." In 1930, perhaps the loveliest of all was finished. The painting remained displayed throughout the years on the walls of the Sun House, in Grace's former studio. Titled simply *The Bride* and numbered "647," the composition is of an unidentified young Pomo bride portrayed in a seated position, surrounded by her dowry of baskets and beads. She gazes pensively into the distance while contemplating her future happiness.

The marriage customs among the Pomo were as varied as the various tribes themselves. An exchange of gifts, however, was common. The marriage itself was not a formal celebration, but an act which solicited public recognition of the two celebrants' union, usually agreed upon in advance by the families involved.

In the days following a marriage, the young couple was invited to take up residence in the home of the girl's mother. For a few days, relatives of the groom brought presents of various kinds to the newlyweds. Then the couple moved to the hut of the groom's parents, and the bride's relatives repeated the gift-giving. Finally, the chief would visit each of the perspective homes and instructed the pair in the marriage customs of the Pomo, while women of the village walked around the houses announcing that a marriage had taken place with a peculiar whistle, called *Sitil*.

In recent years, a few galleries have suggested that many Grace Hudson paintings were subjected to retouching and restoration. When the canvases in question are compared to original photographs taken when the works first were finished, however, few show evidence of alteration. One example is provided by *Ta-cha Ka-wy*, number "548." A lapse of approximately 16 years passed between the start and finish of this painting, if one assumes that Garland Mitchell was drawn when he was actually one year of age. The child was born in 1904, and the painting in question was not finished until 1921.

Possibly the work was not finished until much later because Grace had not been pleased with the start of her effort. On the other hand, the painting may have been produced from an earlier sketch, or reproduced from an original canvas which was destroyed after it served as a model.

. . . . .

From the Bitumen Studies
Private Collection

In the last years of her career, Grace began to turn her thoughts to less serious painting, or just finish previously-started works. Several bitumen sketches were listed in her records along with her far more detailed oil paintings. At least 16 such sketches were numbered by the artist between 1927 and 1928. A large number of canvases painted in the early 1900's had been stored until 1933 in the Sun House. Several of these canvases were included in the numbered paintings of that year, others given only letter designations and not included in Grace's painting diary.

The group represented a commission by the Field Museum to record the Pawnee Indians of Oklahoma. Included in these Hudson paintings are portraits of Eagle Chief, Roam Chief, and their wives. Two profile portraits of Eagle Chief were added to the numbered paintings of 1933 as numbers "660" and "661." Grace wrote:

The museum folks consider Eagle Chief and Roam Chief the two most hand-

some Indians in America. Eagle Chief because of his graceful muscular figure and profound wisdom. Roam Chief was noted for his great height and dignity. Eagle Chief is the brains of the four Pawnee tribes and a number of times he visited Washington D. C. on tribal business. He was received and entertained by the President as an honored guest. The President placed a machine at his disposal and an army officer for a guide and companion. Eagle Chief brought his own interpreter as he spoke no English. For his travels Eagle Chief wears 'almost' civilian clothes but for state dinners, parties, or ceremonial occasions, he dons full dance dress adding only an elaborately embroidered gee string which trails on the ground behind. Beaded moccasins with fringes trailing complete his costume. Eagle Chief's younger brother was a well educated man. He was Roosevelt's secretary in Cuba. One day he told Roosevelt he was tired of fighting with a pencil and wanted to carry a gun and join the ranks. He was among the fallen. President Roosevelt wrote Eagle Chief a letter and sent him a medal in honor of his brother. During his presidency, Roosevelt invited Eagle Chief to the Cowboys' reunions and on two separate occasions as his guest in the White House. The bear is Eagle Chief's symbol. He sings a bear song and dances a bear dance that no one else may perform. He wears the beaded bear's ear in his hair beside the 'breath feather,' a warrior's symbol of vigilance. It is always in motion.

Eagle Chief
Private Collection

Spokaruta lost her father when she was very young. Her mother became a wanderer so Spokaruta was placed in a government school. When she graduated she lived with the Indian agent's family. She was a dainty young lady with her white dresses and her black hair pinned back and was the belle of the ball at the white folk's dances. One day, in the customary was an old woman came to ask Spokaruta's hand for Eagle Chief. The agent's family was indignant but Spokaruta replied, 'I am an Indian, why should I not marry an Indian?' Then they protested he was too old, to which she answered 'He will be more kind than a young man.' Eagle Chief has a large farm, two houses, eight horses and all sorts of vehicles and he purchased a bedroom set and four chairs for his new bride. Spokaruta threw away her hair pins and white folk's clothes and dressed like the other Indians and ate on the floor.

Roam Chief was a very large man. His shoulders were broad and his six feet four inches in height gave him the appearance of a majestic column. His taste in dress is attractive. On ordinary occasions he wears a gorgeous red shirt hanging to his knees trimmed with a little gay colored ribbons flapping in the breeze. A blanket, with a beaded embroidery band through the center, is draped about it. Embroidered moccasins and a glimpse of American trousers complete the costume. He uses green ribbons in his hair and clustered metallic ear rings. At the fair in St. Louis, crowds followed him everywhere when he left the Indian building. In an unusual spirit of ambition, Roam Chief built a two story white house but he soon tired of it and went back to a tent, leaving the house to the woodpeckers.

Mrs. Roam Chief is a happy kindly matron—the envy of all women because her beautiful, big, good natured husband never whips her. Her six children are in the government boarding school. The big house is abandoned so she sits in the little tent and makes beautiful hand embroidered garments with sinew and buckskin.

(l to r) Wife of Eagle Chief, Eagle Chief, Grace Carpenter Hudson, Chief Roan, Wife of Chief Roan

Grace was now on the eve of her 70th birthday. John Hudson was not well and required almost constant attention. What once had been the work of a few weeks or months now took years. The passage of time had not diminished Grace's ability, however, for the few remaining paintings of her career showed no faltering of age or uncertainty of control.

To the last, she continued painting subjects which were as familiar to her as the features of her own hands and face. *Pete McClure and Mollie Duncan,* number

"676," portrayed a scene common to her previous works. A young Tom Mitchell enjoyed a delicious slice of watermelon in painting number "681," while an aged Topsy was painted as a dignified matriarch of the tribe in number "678."

Little by little, the collection of Grace Hudson portraits and paintings was nearing its completion. Grace listed, on the 21st page of her notebook, painting number "683," a sketch of a little girl with a cat-skin shawl draped over her shoulders. The canvas was purchased by actress Janet Gaynor as a Christmas present for one of her friends.

Only after the artist's death were the last two paintings properly attributed. On the back of a painting of a basket baby and dog found in the attic of the Sun House was discovered the number "684." For many years, this painting was believed to have been her last work. Then, much later, further examination of the painting diary revealed that a page had been left blank, while the one following listed an oil sketch of a Pomo boy named Andy, nude, with an eagle feather. Dated December 14, 1935, the sketch was numbered "684," and is believed to have been the last painting executed by Grace Carpenter Hudson.

. . . . .

Dr. John Wilz Napier Hudson died on January 20, 1936; so far as is known, Grace Hudson never painted again. On March 23, 1937, she also died.

In her lifetime, she had preserved a remarkable record of a Native American tribe and had made an even more remarkable contribution to Western Art. Her accomplishment was not limited to that of a documentary, nor was it merely a catalogue of portraits. Grace Carpenter Hudson had searched deep within an Indian people to discover the similarities that bind all men together. "Her Indians," she called them.

As an artist, she stood unique and will never be equalled in her chosen subject. The Pomo tribe that she painted has dwindled and scattered. Many of its legends and traditions exist today only as yellowed bits of paper attached to the canvas of one of her portraits. Through the painted images of Captain John Mewhinney, Topsy, Little Mendocino or Culin, Grace Hudson was able to extend and dignify an entire race of people.

PORTFOLIO

The artist kept a painting diary listing the date of completion, number, dimensions, title, description of each painting; not all paintings, however, contained all information, nor was it alwas listed consistently.

The author has arranged dimensions in proper sequence of height and width whenever necessary. Dimensions are given in inches, followed in parenthesis by the metric equivalent.

Number of a Grace Hudson painting may be determined by examining the back of the canvas. Copyrighted paintings were noted by the designation © over the artist's signature. Dates, when they appear on the canvases, are below the signature.

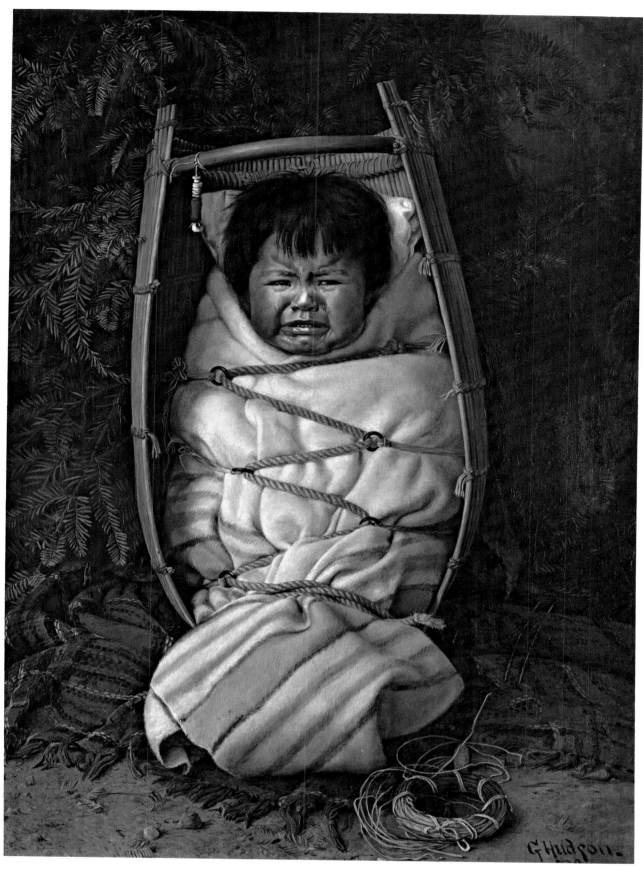

5 Little Mendocino, 1893
36 x 24 (91.4 x 61)
Courtesy California
Historical Society
Louis Sloss Collection

"Little Mendocino is a somewhat daring subject, for short of absolute success it would be ridiculous, but the Indian baby is not ridiculous; it is charm- ing in spite of the fact that it is crying. Everyone admires the little brown thing and longs to comfort it."

28 Who Comes?
   (Cha-ba Wadee), 1894
   30 x 30 (76.2 x 76.2)
   Private collection

"One expects almost momentarily
a view of the intruder and, with
it, to hear a startled cry from
the little occupant of the little
cradle."

20 Yokia Treasures, 1894
38 x 30 (96.5 x 76.2)
Private collection

"The three things most highly
prized by the native Californian
are his child, his basket, and
his dog."

23   The Star (To-tole), 1894
       14 x 10 (35.6 x 25.4)
       Collection of The Oakland
       Museum, Gift of Mrs. Leon
       Chabot Bocqueraz

A young Pomo Indian girl wears a
beautiful headdress with a feather
cluster on top and small ornaments
made from abalone and beads dangling
about her forehead.

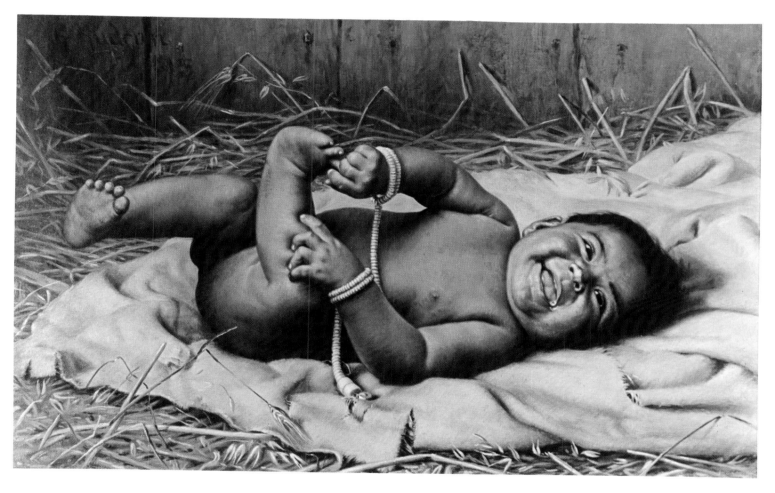

33 My Namesake, 1895
18 x 24 (45.7 x 61)
Private collection

"Before Maggie's baby was born,
she promised to name it after me;
but, as it turned out a boy, it
was called 'Mr. Doctor Hudson Billy-
Bow-legs.' The 'Doctor' was for my
husband and 'Billy-Bow-legs' is
the sobriquet by which the child's
father is known."

98

63 The Boss (Kay Ka-wy), 1896
    30 x 22 (76.2 x 55.9)
    Private collection

To the Pomo mother, the only
treasures in life were her children,
her basketry, and her husband.
From an early age, the male children received much attention, and
The Boss has come to expect his
mother's adoration.

43 Powley, 1895
    17.5 x 10 (44.5 x 25.4)
    Collection of the Los Angeles
    County Museum of Art, Charles
    H. Quinn Bequest

Much of the time, Powley worked for
white settlers, helping them to
plant corn, hops and other crops.

"The cap was fastened to the head with long wooden skewers similar to hat pins. The flicker, or yellow-hammer, quill band was more common. These bands were worn horizontally across the forehead, by both men and women."

61 The Seed Conjurer, 1896
25 x 15 (63.5 x 38.1)
Private collection

81 The Empty Basket, 1897
    18 x 24 (45.7 x 61)
    Private collection

    "Each figure carried some tiny gift
    object as they proceeded single-file
    towards the river to sink the empty
    basket of the departed child."

113 The Orphan, 1898
     32 x 25 (81.3 x 63.5)
     California Historical Society
     Collection

     In the 15 years between the paint-
     ing's completion and the time of its
     sale, the artist altered many of the
     details of the composition of *The
     Orphan*. (See text, page 51.)

114 Help on the Dow, 1898
     Size unknown
     Unknown

     Legend regarding the "Dow," or
     spirit opening, is related to leaving
     an opening in the design of each
     basket so that it may be inspected and
     admired by the spirit of the "basket
     teacher."

155 The Whispering Leaves, 1899   The Pomo Indians believe there is one
     20 x 24 (50.8 x 61)   day in the year when trees have the
     Private collection   power of speech. The messages are open
                                          to all who will pause, reflect and
                                          listen, and can be heard in the flut-
                                          tering and whispering of the falling
                                          leaves.

84 The First Jack, 1897
12 x 8 (30.5 x 20.3)
Private collection

Larger game, such as deer, were
left to the skill of the men.
Boys added to the family food
supply by catching rabbits,
quail and other small animals.

172   Home Care, 1900
      30 x 18.5 (76.2 x 47)
      Unknown

      "Thirty years ago we did not
      realize that the Indian was not
      to be with us always."

177   Head of John Jake's Father
      (Kol-ba), 1900
      12 x 8 (30.5 x 20.3)
      California Historical Society

The Medicine man, Kol-ba, held
an important office. He cured the
sick, helped drive bad spirits
from the mad, and was always noted
for his beautiful garments.

149 Yesterday, 1899
     14 x 10.5 (35.6 x 26.7)
     Private collection

Even by the time of Grace Hudson's
painting, the traditional Indian
dress had passed into white-men's
clothing.

106

186 Hawaiian Girl, 1901
20 x 16 (50.8 x 40.6)
Private collection

Young Hawaiian woman, sixteen
to twenty years old, with two
ilina leis. Her hair is short and
casually combed.

196 Mary Low Eating Poi
(A Kam Aaima), 1902
24 x 28 (61 x 71.1)
Unknown

"A native child, frowsy-headed and
bright-eyed, is kneeling in ecstasy
over a calabash of poi from which
she is eating with her finger, after
the fashion of the most-approved table
manners of the Hawaiians."

209 Old Hawaiian Woman, 1901
    7 x 5 (17.8 x 12.7)
    Private collection

An old, white-haired Hawaiian woman.

187 Lei Girl, 1901
    29 x 24 (73.7 x 61)
    Private collection

A common sight on the streets of
turn of the century Honolulu was the
colorful lei maker.

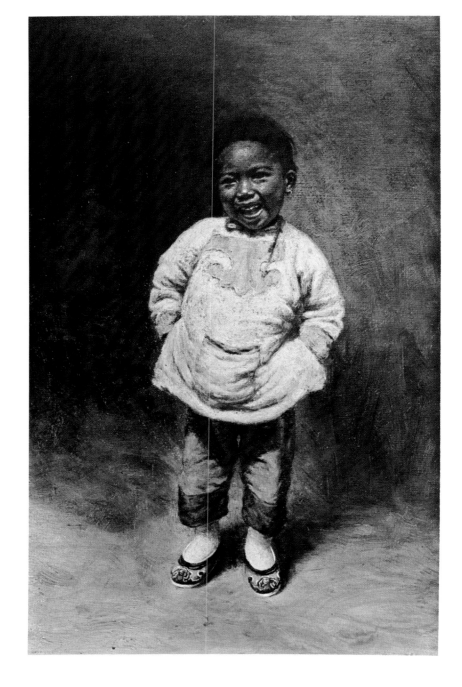

188 Chinese Girl Laughing, 1901
    9 x 6 (22.9 x 15.2)
    Private collection

As Grace returned to her artwork in
Hawaii, a series of colorful island
children emerged from her canvas.

212 The Dowry, 1902
     25 x 30 (63.5 x 76.2)
     Private collection

     "The Indian bride is decked in her
     best shawl and beads, and holds in
     her hand the most valued of her
     treasures. It is the smallest
     basket, and into its reeds are
     woven feathers and abalone and bead
     pendants."

277 The Comforter, 1905
     27 x 20 (68.6 x 50.8)
     Unknown

     Angel is holding her little
     brother in her arms.

268 Indian Summer, 1905
    20 x 16 (50.8 x 40.6)
    Unknown

Eva, young Indian woman, wearing a
dress open to the waist is standing in
a large field holding a tar-weed gatherer.
To her left side is a cone shaped basket.

255 Found in the Brush
(Ka-mo-Ki-yu), 1904
23 x 34 (58.4 x 36.4)
Los Angeles Athletic
Club Collection

It was common for the Pomo women
to describe their first children
as "being found in the brush."
It portended great achievements
for the young.

346 Boy with Ducklings, 1909
8 x 10 (20.3 x 25.4)
Private collection

For a long time, the little boy had
visited the hen, patiently waiting
for the birth of his duck eggs.

330 The Little One (Chuly), 1908
30 x 36 (76.2 x 91.4)
Private collection

Pomos are very fond of children. A
woman who has a baby will spend
practically all of her time playing
with it, and will not think of making
a basket or doing any work.

309 The Mystic Symbol, 1907
   30 x 30 (76.2 x 76.2)
   Private collection

"The quail woman" who taught the
Indians basketry bade them use certain
symbols for her that she might come
at any time and go from top to bottom
of the basket and inspect the work.

407 Portrait of Pomo Chief, 1912
20 x 15 (50.8 x 38.1)
Private collection

Kay-will, chief of one of the
Pomo tribes, was a frequent sitter
for the artist's canvases.

378 The Basket Maker, 1911
22 x 18 (55.9 x 45.7)
Private collection

Like many coastal California tribes,
the Pomo's women excelled in basketry.
Some baskets were woven smaller
than a dime, others with as many as
65 stitches per inch.

448 The Pilferer (Ma-Ka), 1914
     22 x 16 (55.9 x 40.6)
     Private collection

     The Matu woods were a fine place
     for finding pretty treasures.

337 Trouble (Pi-shu-din), 1909
     20 x 16 (50.8 x 40.6)
     Unknown

     Many of Grace Hudson's paintings
     left little doubt in the viewer's
     mind as to the outcome. Trouble
     indeed—and who could doubt it?

381 Little Girl, 1911
     10 x 8 (25.4 x 20.3)
     Private collection

The California poppy was a forbidden flower to the Pomo youngsters. Despite her parent's warnings,
the Little Girl just could not
stay away from the golden blooms.

452 The Lonesome Hour, 1914
28.25 x 21.75 (71.8 x 55.2)
Private collection

The hour between sunset and dark was a lonely time for a Mai-du bride among the Pomos. Her only guests were her own people who came to visit her. When the women work, she worked alone, with only her husband to think well of her.

420   Little Woman
      (Mad-tha-koo), 1912
      Size unknown
      Private collection

419 Col-lip-win, 1912
    18 x 12 (45.7 x 30.5)
    Private collection

Mad-tha-koo (above) and the wandering fisherboy represented the Pomo adolescents to Grace Hudson. Col-lip-win wandered about fishing. He stayed with relatives or friends, or even strangers, wherever he could find shelter.

121

"I was at the river sketching a
summer camp when little Kol-ba came
running home calling, 'I got a
fish!' "

465 Tale-O with Squirrels, 1915
20 x 16 (50.8 x 40.6)
Private collection

"The Indians are especially fond of
squirrels or any game. The old folks
say that the reason the tribe is
dying is because they are compelled to
eat beef and flour instead of fish,
game, acorns, buckeyes, wild bulbs and
tubers, shell fish and sea-weed,
salt from the ocean and sugar from
the pine tree."

124

492 The Dove Place (Ma-yu-ma), 1917
24 x 19 (61 x 48.3)
Private collection

Sharing with the birds of the sky.

477 Hark that Squirrel
(Sho-ma-ma-begay), 1916
20 x 16 (50.8 x 40.6)
Private collection

Boy and dog, the inseparable Pomo
pair.

461 Pomo Children and a Dog in the
Rain, 1915
24 x 18 (61 x 45.7)
Private collection

Makila Madtha, the rain woman,
rises in the east seeking Makila,
the thunderman.

478 The War Eagle (Shai), 1916
     27 x 20 (68.6 x 50.8)
     Private collection

"The widow Ket-si-om and her Gemini
on the way to the quail traps discover Shai, the War Eagle, soaring
above them. They pause and watch
knowing that if Shai drops a feather
it is for Gemini and presages his
strength and greatness."

495 The Chipmunk, 1917
16 x 20 (40.6 x 50.8)
Unknown

Bat-sim-tsi lives near the Indian
hut and, as Culin daily feeds him, he
grows fatter and bolder.

479 The Little Jack, 1916
12.5 x 12.5 (54.6 x 31.8)
Unknown

The jackrabbit—like every other
animal and bird, retains the reputation
established in legend. In Pomo myth,
the rabbit helped his human
brothers find fire.

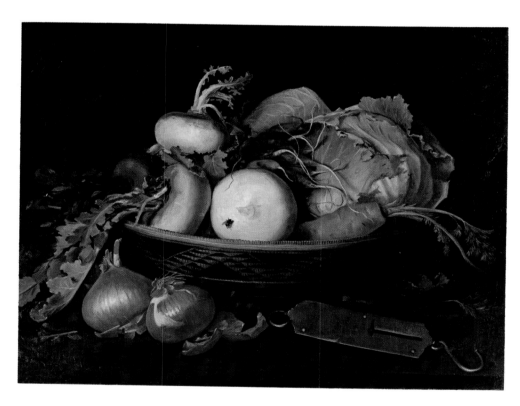

N.A. Still life
Date unknown
17 x 22 (43.2 x 55.9)
Private collection

Rarely, Grace Hudson demonstrated her
talent for painting other than human
subjects. Perhaps nowhere was this
better demonstrated than the still
life shown here.

129

498 Ray of Light (Da-ta-leu), 1917
16 x 10 (40.6 x 25.4)
Private collection

When she was a maiden, Da-ta-leu's
mother was sent to government school.
She returned wishing that she was
not an Indian, but ma-san, or
white. Her child's birth brought
her heart back to the tribe and,
in grateful thanks, she named her
Ray of Light.

499 Gimini, 1917
16 x 13.5 (40.6 x 34.3)
Unknown

"Gimini and his mother
live by themselves in a little
shack on the mountainside.
Gimini has neither playmates
nor toys, only the ducks
that he has raised with the
help of the kindly hen."

130

131

511 The Oracle of the Leaves
August 14, 1918
24.5 x 20 (62.2 x 50.8)
Private collection

Girls and wives of the Pomo
lingered in the forest to
hear the leaves speak, each
seeking the answer to the
wish of her heart.

525 Hu-hi-ya and Bu-shay, 1919
20 x 16 (50.8 x 40.6)
Private collection

"One day while Hu-hi-ya was sitting
very still watching a squirrel, the
tiny bu-shay walked straight up to
her and said, 'Take me home!' "

502 A Hold Up, August 20, 1917
20 x 17 (50.8 x 43.2)
Unknown

"Little Du-wee, getting hungry,
comes back to camp for some bread,
but the hen and chickens feel they
own a common interest."

537 Our Home (Yath Chow), 1920
16 x 22 (40.6 x 55.9)
Private collection

The old Pomo wampum maker, John Scott,
and Eva before the men's sweathouse
at Guidiville.

135

554   Untitled, 1922
      16 x 11 (40.6 x 27.9)
      Private collection

      "Ka-tat believes the ways of his
      father's are good enough for him."

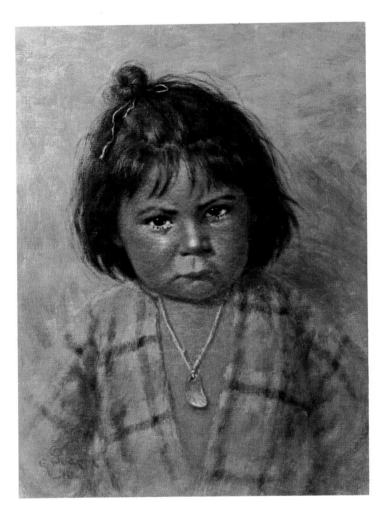

514   Du-ko-li, November 26, 1918
      14 x 10 (35.6 x 25.4)
      Private collection

      "After Wy-lakki John's death,
      his son and little grand daughter
      [sic] Du-co-li left Round Valley to
      wander from tribe to tribe seeking
      a welcome. The man and little
      girl are always alone, here and
      there and everywhere like gypsies."

548   Stranger Baby
      (Ya-cha Ka-wy), 1921
      14 x 10 (35.6 x 25.4)
      Private collection

      "The Indians are ever clannish.
      Though he lives among them
      in amity and participates in
      their ceremonies, he is still
      Ya-cha, a stranger, and his
      baby is Ya-cha Ka-wy."

137

560 The Betrothed, 1922
22 x 16 (55.9 x 40.6)
Private collection

"Pomo marriages are arranged
by the parents or oldest
male relative after the young
man selects his bride. Ta-le-a
has just received her betrothal
gifts but has not seen the man
who has chosen her for his wife.

590 Rosa, 1924
27.5 x 25.5 (69.9 x 64.8)
Private collection

Rosa was the Indian saint after
which the northern California
town of Santa Rosa was named.
Father Juan Amoroso baptized the
child in the stream which
flowed at their feet.

561 The Grandchildren, 1922
20 x 16 (50.8 x 40.6)
Private collection

Kol-ta-bish and Lote snuggle down
by a tree until Ja-kum's wife's
basket is filled.

533 The Foxes (Kole-pi-ta), 1919
24 x 18 (61 x 45.7)
Private collection

When Kole-pi-ta had measles,
she was peevish, restless and
hard to please, until old grand-
father brought in a fox 'kitten.'
By the time Kole-pi-ta had recovered, the fox was named
Con-cu and established as a
member of the family under the
protection of her indulgent
parents.

622 Tullo's boy Dubert, 1928
20.5 x 15.5 (52 x 39.4)
Private collection

Indians are fond of pets and
often bring the infant animals
home for playmates for the
children.

141

619 Helen (Qui-tak-tak
Kol-di-le), 1927
10 x 14 (25.4 x 35.6)
Private collection

"Through the long summer days
the grassy hillside is a beautiful garden to the bugs, the
bees, the butterflies, and
Kol-si."

609 Eyes of the Highway, 1927
16 x 12 (40.6 x 30.5)
Private collection

Far from civilization and however solitary the traveler
may feel, there are always
eyes watching. It may be the
eyes of a bird, a rabbit, a
panther, or only a little Indian boy and his dog playing
in a clump of flowers.

601 Two Indian Children
   (Kati-brin and Ka-tum), 1926
   24 x 22 (61 x 55.9)
   Private collection

"The Jay's sharp eyes and
ears are always near the
children and his loud chatter
tells of their misdeeds."

652 It is a Good World
(Betoom), 1931
16 x 12 (40.6 x 30.5)
Private collection

"Life is still young and sweet
in a little valley just over the
hill from the great Highway."

580 When the Birds Went to War
(Kal-Pin), 1923
Size unknown
Unknown

"In each Pomo village there
were one or more old men whose
duty and pleasure it was to
preserve intact the traditions
of the tribe and to teach them
to the younger generation."

613 Left Behind (Kol-piu), 1927
14 x 10 (35.6 x 25.4)
Private collection

"To come to town every week
is the great event in an
Indian household."

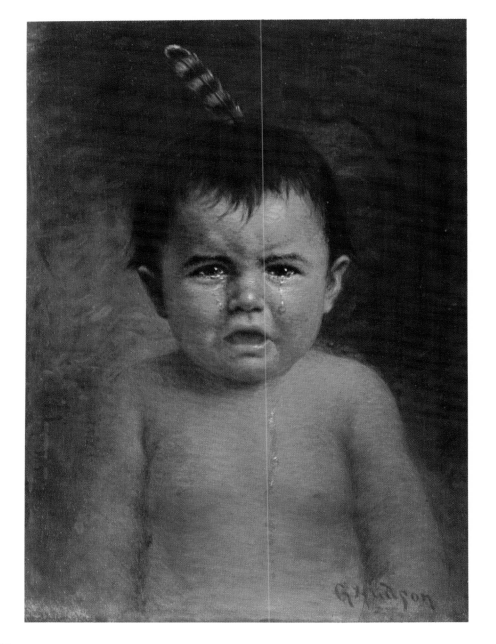

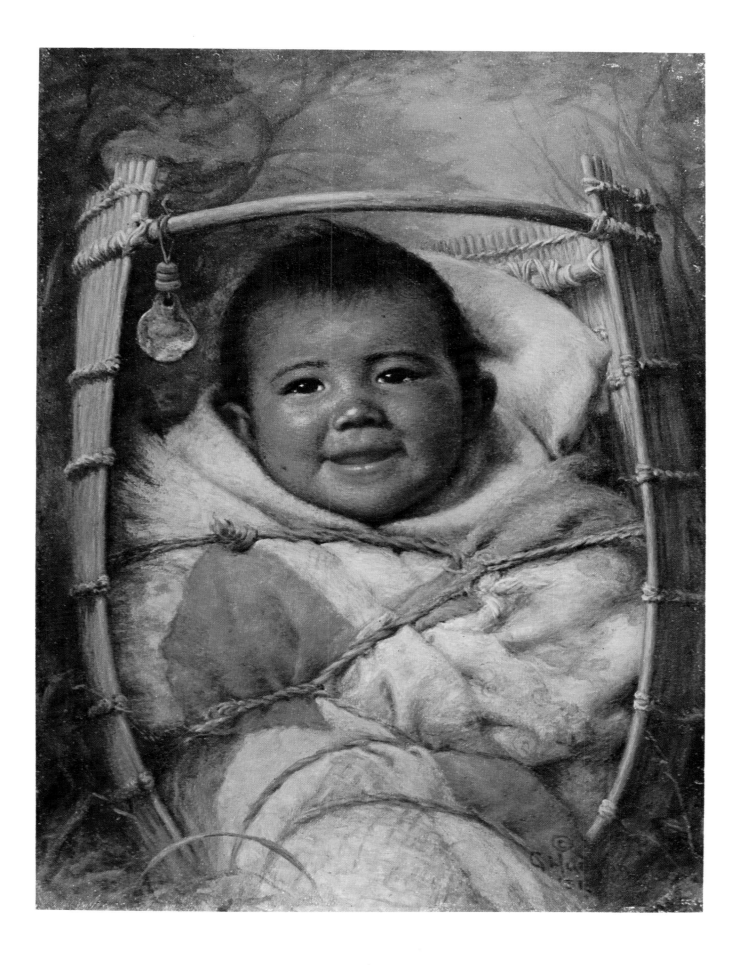

536 The Rain Doll (Shaili), 1920
21 x 16 (53.3 x 40.6)
Unknown

"Prominently wearing the
paraphenalia for the ceremony
is Pa-da, the rain doll, a
small pointed slab of wood,
carved and decorated. As the
priests pray with rain dolls,
the men make rain dolls as
symbolic toys for their favored
sons."

598 The Good Old Summer Time 1925
17 x 11 (43.2 x 27.9)
Private collection

Hop picking is the great social
and financial season in the
Indian's year. The tribes
mingle and gather in the work,
and Kol-pin has the candy that
he was promised all winter.

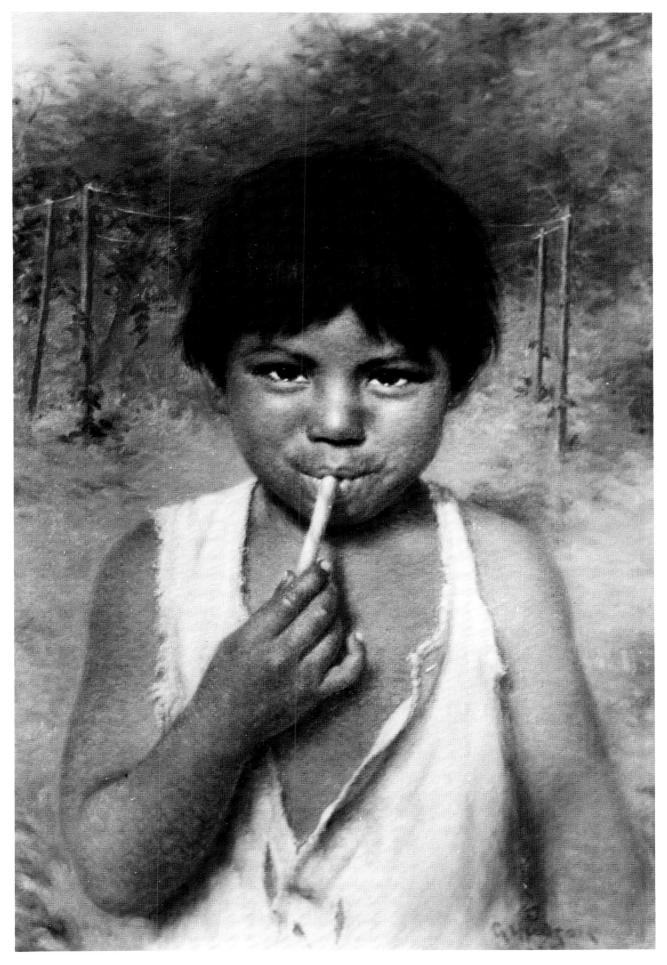

147

647　The Bride, 1930
24.5 x 20 (62.2 x 50.8)
Private collection

The Indian bride, surrounded
by gifts from both families,
pauses to reflect on the
future.

656　The Dawn of Song (La-mu), 1932
20.5 x 26.5 (52 x 67.3)
Ukiah Public Library collection

"Having been so long in darkness, it was a quiet world with
only the sounds of the night,
the falling of a bough, the
rolling of a stone or the
angry growl of an animal, till
La-mu, the Gopher man, discovered sweet notes in the hollow stem of the elderberry
tree."

148

637 Kay-will, 1928
     20 x 16 (50.8 x 40.6)
     Private collection

Kay-will was the last of the
old hereditary chiefs of the
Pomos.

636 Holy Mary, 1928
     20 x 16 (50.8 x 40.6)
     Private collection

Ba-dai was a comely brown maid-
en when the white settlers came.
Today she is a helpless old woman, living in a little hut with
her last surviving relative, a
small grandson."

152

678 Topsy (Kol-pi-ta), 1934
35 x 18 (88.9 x 45.7)
Private collection

"She was the last of the old
line Indian Medicine women, and
I do not believe there will
be another to take her place.
Ideas, even among the Indians,
are changing rapidly these
days."

676 Cha-bok and Kay-kay-pun, 1934
18 x 24 (45.7 x 61)
Private collection

Seated in front of the sweathouse
making "Indian gold," or wampum, and baskets are two elderly
Indians.

153

681 Boy with Watermelon, 1935
16 x 12 (40.6 x 30.5)
Private collection

Some things brought by the
white men found acceptance
among the Indians.

581 The Basket Maker, 1923
12 x 16 (30.5 x 40.6)
Private collection

The Pomo are noted as the makers
of the most beautiful baskets.
A basket is the Indian's cradle,
utensil, chest, jewel and funeral gift.

154

684 Basket Baby, 1935
     18 x 10 (45.7 x 25.4)
     Private collection

Like her first, Grace Hudson's
next to last painting dealt
with the universal image of
Pomo Indian youth—the basket
baby and his dog.

1 National Thorn
1891
30 x 30 (76.2 x 76.2)
Unknown

2 Belle of the Tribe
Katum
1892
23½ x 18 (56.7 x 45.7)
Private Collection

3 Captain John Mewhinney
1892
22 x 17 (55.9 x 43.2)
National Portrait Gallery

4 The Interrupted Bath
Quail Baby
1892
Unknown
Unknown

5 Little Mendocino
1893
36 x 24 (91.4 x 61)
Private Collection

6 None
1893
Unknown
Unknown

7 None
1893
Unknown
Unknown

8 None
1893
Unknown
Unknown

9 None
1893
Unknown
Unknown

10 Unknown
1893
Unknown
Unknown

11 None
1893
Unknown
Unknown

12 None
1893
Unknown
Unknown

13 Unknown
1893
Unknown
Private collection

14 Unknown
1893
Unknown

15 "Billy Kept Plump"
1893
6 x 4 (15.2 x 10.2)
Unknown

16 Katum
1893
Small panel
Unknown

17 "Turnip baby"
1893
35½ x 28½ (90.2 x 72.4)
Private collection

18 "Lonesome"
1894
Small
Unknown

19 "Apple baby"
1894
4½ x 5 (11.4 x 12.7)
Private collection

20 "Yokia Treasures"
1894
38 x 30 (96.5 x 76.2)
Unknown

21 "Disappointment"
1894
Unknown
Unknown

22 None
1894
5½ x 4 (14 x 10.2)
Unknown

23 "To-tole"
1894
14 x 10 (35.6 x 25.4)
Oakland Museum

24 "Baby Bunting"
1894
31 x 30 (78.7 x 76.2)
Private collection

25 None
1894
7 x 4 (17.8 x 10.2)
Unknown

26 None
1894
7 x 4 (17.8 x 10.2)
Unknown

27 None
1894
8 x 5½ (20.3 x 14)
Unknown

28 "Cho-ba wah-dee"?
(Who comes)
1894
30 x 30 (76.2 x 76.2)
Unknown

29 "Mama!"
1894
15 x 12 (38.1 x 30.5)
Destroyed

30 "Early birds"
1894
Unknown
Unknown

31 "Jimmie"
1895
18 x 14 (45.7 x 35.6)
Private collection

32 Diffidence
1895
None
Unknown

33 "My Name-sake"
1895
18 x 24 (45.7 x 61)
Private collection

34 "Little Piper"
1895
10 x 6 (25.4 x 15.2)
Unknown

35 None
1895
7 x 7½ (17.8 x 19.1)
Private collection

36 "Rosie"
1895
14 x 10 (35.6 x 25.4)
Unknown

37 None
1895
8 x 5½ (20.3 x 14)
Private collection

38 None
1895
6 x 10 (15.2 x 25.4)
Unknown

39 None
1895
7 x 5 (17.8 x 12.7)
Unknown

40 "Powley's Sweetheart"
1895
17 x 10 (43.2 x 25.4)
Unknown

41 "The First Pang"
1895
Unknown
Destroyed

42 "Mr. Hudson".
1895
10 x 8 (25.4 x 20.3)
Unknown

43 "Powley"
1895
17½ x 10 (44.5 x 25.4)
Unknown

44 None
1895
7½ x 5½ (19.1 x 14)
Unknown

45 "Mendocino Products"
1895
13 x 25 (33 x 63.5)
Unknown

46 "Lonesome"
1895
10 x 8 (25.4 x 20.3)
Unknown

47 "Tis a sad, sad, world"
1895
12 x 15 (30.5 x 38.1)
Unknown

48 None
1895
12 x 8 (30.5 x 20.3)
Unknown

49 None
1895
9 x 7 ((22.9 x 17.8)
Unknown

50 Rosa
1895
14 x 10 (35.6 x 25.4)
Unknown

51 "Lucky Head"
    1895
    8 x 6 (20.3 x 15.2)
    Unknown

52 Mr. Hudson
    1895
    8 x 6 (20.3 x 15.2)
    Unknown

53 Annis
    1895
    11 x 8 (28 x 20.3)
    Unknown

54 None
    1896
    12 x 8 (30.5 x 20.3)
    Unknown

55 "Kal–Katum"
    Mollie
    1896
    17 x 14 (43.2 x 35.6)
    Unknown

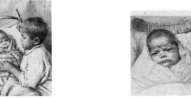

56 May Ellis
    1896
    10 x 8 (25.4 x 20.3)
    Private collection

57 "Little brother"
    1896
    15 x 12 (38.1 x 30.5)
    Unknown

58 Burnam
    1896
    8½ x 8 (21.6 x 20.3)
    Unknown

59 None
    1896
    8 x 6 (20.3 x 15.2)
    Unknown

60 None
    1896
    9 x 6 (22.9 x 15.2)
    Unknown

61 "The Seed Conjurer"
    1896
    25 x 15 (63.5 x 38.1)
    Private collection

62 Greenie
    1896
    8 x 10 (20.3 x 25.4)
    Unknown

63 "Kay Kah-wy"
    (The Boss)
    1896
    30 x 22 Oval (76.2 x 55.9)
    Private collection

64 "Pomo Dancer"
    1896
    24 x 18 (61 x 45.7)
    Unknown

65 "Mr. Hudson"
    1896
    9 x 5½ (22.9 x 14)
    Private collection

66 "Blue Monday"
    1896
    38 x 30 (96.5 x 76.2)
    Unknown

67 "The Tar-weed Gatherer"
    1896
    23 x 13 (58.4 x 33)
    Private collection

68 Lu's baby
    1896
    10 x 8 (25.4 x 20.3)
    Unknown

69 "Quail Hunter"
    1896
    30 x 20 Oval (76.2 x 50.8)
    Private collection

70 "The Baby"
    1896
    5 x 6 (12.7 x 15.2)
    Unknown

71 Girl yawning
    1896
    14 x 10 (35.6 x 25.4)
    Unknown

72 "The Runaway"
    1896
    30 x 22 (76.2 x 55.9)
    Unknown

73 Greenie with two yellow
      puppies
    1896
    10 x 8 (25.4 x 20.3)
    Unknown

74 Burnam
    1896
    4 x 5 (10.2 x 12.7)
    Unknown

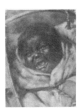

75 "Mr. Hudson"
    1896
    Round 12" Diameter (30.5)
    Unknown

76 None
1896
7 x 5½ (17.8 x 14)
Unknown

77 None
1896
4¾ x 4 (12.1 x 10.2)
Unknown

78 "Let's Make up!"
1897
28 x 38 (71.1 x 96.5)
Unknown

79 Baby Fitch
1897
Round 12" diameter (30.5)
Unknown

80 None
1897
3½ x 2½ Oval (8.9 x 6.4)
Unknown

81 "Return from Funeral"
1897
18 x 24 (45.7 x 61)
Private collection

82 "Knights of the Forest"
1897
32 x 25 (81.3 x 63.5)
Destroyed

83 Child Holding Black
Puppy
Unknown
11½ x 8 (29.2 x 20.3)
Private collection

84 "The First Jack"
1897
12 x 8 (30.5 x 20.3)
Private collection

85 Burnam
1897
Round 6" diameter (15.2)
Unknown

86 None
1897
12 x 8 (30.5 x 20.3)
Unknown

87 Burnam
1897
7½ x 10 (19.1 x 25.4)
Unknown

88 "Annie"
1897
12 x 9 (30.5 x 22.9)
Unknown

89 "Mr. Hudson"
1897
5½ x 8 (14 x 20.3)
Private collection

90 "Annis"
1897
Round 4" diameter (10.2)
Private collection

91 None
1897
12 x 8 (30.5 x 20.3)
Unknown

92 Grace Carpenter
1897
10 x 8 (25.4 x 20.3)
Private collection

93 None
1897
Round, 4" diameter (10.2)
Unknown

94 None
1897
10 x 7½ (25.4 x 19.1)
Unknown

95 None
1897
7 x 4¼ (17.8 x 10.8)
Private collection

96 "The Skeptic"
1897
20 x 27 (50.8 x 68.6)
Unknown

97 "A Native Wild Flower"
1897
8½ x 6 Oval (21.6 x 15.2)
Unknown

98 None
1897
4 x 5½ (10.2 x 14)
Unknown

99 "Hogs"
1897
Round 6" diameter (15.2)
Private collection

100 None
1897
8 x 12 (20.3 x 30.5)
Unknown

101 "Baggage"
1897
25 x 32 (63.5 x 81.3)
Unknown

102 None
1897
5½ x 3¾ (14 x 9.5)
Unknown

103 Burnham in Red Shirt
1897
8 x 6 Oval (20.3 x 15.2)
Unknown

104 Jennie's Tom Smoking
1897
15½ x 11 (39.4 x 27.9)
Private collection

105 Monk's Wife
1897
8 x 6 (20.3 x 15.2)
Unknown

106 Tullo
(Thurlow Mitchell)
1897
5½ x 5 (14 x 12.7)
Private collection

107 None
1897
5½ x 4½ (14 x 11.4)
Unknown

108 Burnham in Red Shirt
1897
8" diameter (20.3)
Unknown

109 Coming of the Coyote
(De-Wy Bu-Sh)
1898
24 x 18 (61 x 45.7)
Private collection

110 None
1898
4½ x 5½ (11.4 x 14)
Unknown

111 Belle
1898
15 x 12 (38.1 x 30.5)
Unknown

112 Black Bird
(Tsu-Li-Ya)
1898
5½ x 4 (14 x 10.2)
Private collection

113 "The Orphan"
1898
32 x 25 (81.3 x 63.5)
California Historical Society

114 "Help on Dav"
1898
16 x 24 (40.6 x 61)
Unknown

115 Thurlow
1898
9½ x 7 (24 x 17.8)
Unknown

116 Tom with Jack Rabbit
1898
9½ x 7 (24 x 17.8)
Unknown

117 Nettie
1898
8" diameter (Round) (20.3)
Unknown

118 None
1898
6½ x 4½ (16.5 x 11.4)
Private collection

119 Love's Labor
1898
12 x 15 (30.5 x 38.1)
Private collection

120 Old John
1898
9¼ x 7½ (23.5 x 19.1)
Private collection

121 Burnham
(Tso)
1898
6 x 7½ (15.2 x 19.1)
Private collection

122 Thurlow Creeping
1898
6½ x 5½ (16.5 x 14)
Unknown

123 Back to Her Tribe
1898
27 x 20 (68.6 x 50.8)
Private collection

124 None
1898
4 x 6½ (10.2 x 16.5)
Unknown

125 Jennie
1898
7½ x 5 (19.1 x 12.7)
Unknown

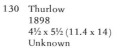

126 Delia's Boy
1898
8 x 5 (20.3 x 12.7)
Private collection

127 Emmet
1898
7 x 5 (17.8 x 12.7)
Unknown

128 Emmet
1898
6 x 6 (15.2 x 15.2)
Unknown

129 Thurlow
1898
6 x 6 (15.2 x 15.2)
Unknown

130 Thurlow
1898
4½ x 5½ (11.4 x 14)
Unknown

131 Belle
1898
10 x 8 (25.4 x 20.3)
Unknown

132 Wiskey Jennie
1898
8 x 5¾ (20.3 x 14.6)
Private collection

133 Ju-De-La
1898
8 x 6 (20.3 x 15.2)
Unknown

134 Bride
(Bah-Sho)
1898
20 x 14 (50.8 x 35.6)
Private collection

135 Bride
1898
20 x 14 (50.8 x 35.6)
Private collection

136 Dancer
1898
33 x 23 (83.8 x 58.4)
Private collection

137 Old Captain Bill
(Lau-Nau)
1898
8 x 6 (20.3 x 15.2)
Private collection

138 Captain Charley
(Chief Ploom)
1898
9½ x 6 (24.1 x 15.2)
Unknown

139 Old Couple
(Ko-Di-Na)
1898
12 x 16 (30.5 x 40.6)
Unknown

140 Captain Bill
(Lav-Hav)
1898
8½ x 6 (21.6 x 15.2)
Unknown

141 Thurlow
1898
7¼ x 7¼ (18.4 x 18.4)
Unknown

142 Close Friends
(Wi-Na-Wa)
1898
12 x 15 (30.5 x 38.1)
Private collection

143 Nora—A Dancer
1898
20 x 14 (50.8 x 35.6)
Private collection

144 None
1898
6½ x 4¾ (16.5 x 12.1)
Unknown

145 "Cornered"
(Burnham)
1898
6½ x 4¼ (16.5 x 10.8)
Unknown

146 Hudson Mitchell
1898
6½ x 6½ (16.5 x 16.5)
Unknown

147 While The Hop Ripen
1898
20 x 14 (50.8 x 35.6)
Destroyed

148 Today
1898
14 x 10½ (35.6 x 26.7)
Destroyed

149 Yesterday
1898
14 x 10½ (35.6 x 26.7)
Private collection

150 Tom Mitchell's Girl Annie
1898
7½ x 7½ (19.1 x 19.1)
Unknown

151 The Good Aunt
1898
20 x 15 (50.8 x 38.1)
Unknown

152 None
1898
9 x 6 (22.9 x 15.2)
Private collection

153 Thurlow
1898
7½ x 5½ (19.1 x 14)
Unknown

154 None
1898
4½ x 6½ (11.4 x 16.5)
Unknown

155 "The Whispering Leaves"
1900
20 x 24 (50.8 x 61)
Private collection

156 Lu's Baby
1900
5½ x 4½ (14 x 11.4)
Unknown

157 Thurlow in the Lupins
1900
6 x 8 (15.2 x 20.3)
Unknown

158 Trade Day
1900
20 x 15 (50.8 x 38.1)
Destroyed

159 Thurlow
1900
5 x 6½ (12.7 x 16.5)
Private collection

160 Thurlow
1900
6½ x 5 (16.5 x 12.7)
Unknown

161 Annie
1900
6½ x 5½ (16.5 x 14)
Destroyed

162 A Diplomat
1900
14 x 14 (35.6 x 25.6)
Unknown

163 Potter's Little Girl
(Shu-Sett)
1900
4½ x 5½ (11.4 x 14)
Unknown

164 Potter's Little Girl
1900
6 x 5 (15.2 x 12.7)
Private collection

165 Annie
1900
6 x 4½ (15.2 x 11.4)
Unknown

166 Mollie's Baby
1900
5½ x 6¾ (14 x 17.2)
Unknown

167 None
1900
6½ x 5 (16.5 x 12.7)
Unknown

168 None
1900
5½ x 7½ (14 x 19.1)
Unknown

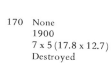

169 Annie
1900
27 x 20 (68.6 x 50.8)
Private collection

170 None
1900
7 x 5 (17.8 x 12.7)
Destroyed

171 Sadie
1900
8½ x 5 (21.6 x 12.7)
Destroyed

172 Home Care
(Myrt)
1900
30 x 18½ (76.2 x 47)
Unknown

173 Annie
1900
7 x 5 (17.8 x 12.7)
Unknown

174 Fitch Baby
1900
2¾ x 3 (7 x 7.6)
Unknown

175 None
1900
5½ x 7 (14 x 17.8)
Unknown

176 Carlos Baby
1900
6½ x 5 (16.5 x 12.7)
Unknown

177 Kol-Ba
1900
12 x 8 (30.5 x 20.3)
Private collection

178 Puppies
1900
7 x 4 (17.8 x 10.2)
Private collection

179 Thurlow
1900
5½ x 5 (14 x 12.7)
Unknown

180 Knight Baby
1900
6 x 6½ (15.2 x 16.5)
Unknown

181 None
1900
7½ x 5 (19.1 x 12.7)
Private collection

182 Johnson Child With Cat
1900
6 x 4 (15.2 x 10.2)
Unknown

183 Coon's Girl Jennie
1900
7½ x 5 (19.1 x 12.7)
Private collection

184 Annie
(Little Shy Eagle)
1900
None
Private collection

185 Japanese Baby
1901
4 x 4 (10.2 x 10.2)
Private collection

186 Hawaiian Girl
1901
20 x 16 (50.8 x 40.6)
Private collection

187 Lei Girl
1901
29 x 24 (73.7 x 61)
Private collection

188 Laughing Chinese Girl
1901
9 x 6 (22.9 x 15.2)
Private collection

189 Chinese Child
1901
6 x 5 (15.2 x 12.7)
Unknown

190 Hawaiian Women
1901
20 x 16 (50.8 x 40.6)
Destroyed

191 Hawaiian Child
1901
6 x 5 (15.2 x 12.7)
Destroyed

192 Regret
(Minaniaa)
1901
20 x 16 (50.8 x 40.6)
Private collection

193 Bramble Bush
(Kokalaoa)
1901
4 x 3 (10.2 x 7.6)
Unknown

194 Nui Nui
1901
19 x 15 (48.3 x 38.1)
Private collection

195 Girl With Beads
1901
19 x 15 (48.3 x 38.1)
Private collection

196 Mary Low Eating Poi
(A-Kam-Aaima)
24 x 28 (61 x 71.1)
Unknown

197 Pets
(Punaheli)
1901
8 x 5 (20.3 x 12.7)
Unknown

198 None
1901
4½ x 3 (11.4 x 7.6)
Private collection

199 Hawaiian Boy
1901
11½ x 15 (29.2 x 38.1)
Private collection

200 Hawaiian Child
1901
7½ x 5 (19.1 x 12.7)
Unknown

201 Hawaiian Child
1901
5 x 6 (12.7 x 15.2)
Private collection

202 Hawaiian Child
1901
11 x 15 (27.9 x 38.1)
Unknown

203 Hawaiian Child
(Box)
1901
7½ x 5 (19.1 x 12.7)
Private collection

204 Rosa's Baby
1901
6½ x 5½ (16.5 x 14)
Private collection

205 Lowe
1901
7 x 4¼ (17.8 x 10.8)
Private collection

206 Hapa Naoli
1901
20 x 16 (50.8 x 40.6)
Private collection

207 The Beautiful
(Leu Mi Gayo)
1901
8 x 6 (20.3 x 15.2)
Unknown

208 Katu
1901
Unknown
Private collection

209 Hawaiian Women
1901
7 x 5 (17.8 x 12.7)
Private collection

210 Hawaiian Woman
(Hilo)
1901
20 x 16 (50.8 x 40.6)
Unknown

211 Hilo Girl
1901
7 x 5 (17.8 x 12.7)
Destroyed

212 The Dowry
1902
25 x 30 (63.5 x 76.2)
Private collection

213 Annie
1902
9 x 6½ (22.9 x 16.5)
Unknown

214 Tijon Boy
1902
9 x 3¼ (22.9 x 8.3)
Unknown

215 Thurlow
1902
6½ x 3¾ (16.5 x 9.5)
Private collection

216 "Willium"
1902
7¼ x 5½ (18.4 x 14.0)
Unknown

217 Tijon Girl
1902
3½ x 7 (8.9 x 17.8)
Unknown

218 Tijon Child With Basket
1902
Unknown
Unknown

219 Lusanna
1902
20 x 15 (50.8 x 38.1)
Private collection

220 Little Woman
(Mad-Tha-Coo)
36 x 21 (91.4 x 53.3)
Private collection

221 Pawnee Boy
1902
11 x 14 (27.9 x 35.6)
Unknown

222 None
1902
5 x 5 (12.7 x 12.7)
Private collection

223 A Treasure
1902
6 x 5¼ (15.2 x 13.3)
Coe Kerr Gallery Inc.

224 None
1902
5½ x 4½ (14 x 11.4)
Unknown

225 Rosa's Baby
1902
6 x 5 (15.2 x 12.7)
Private collection

226 Ma-Yu
1903
20 x 15 (50.8 x 38.1)
Unknown

227 Eagle Chief's Daughter
1903
7 x 5 (17.8 x 12.7)
Unknown

228 Chi-Ka-Ka
1903
20 x 15 (50.8 x 38.1)
Private collection

229 None
1903
6¼ x 5¼ (15.9 x 13.3)
Private collection

230 Sweethearts
1903
20 x 27 (50.8 x 68.6)
Private collection

231 Of The Mountain People
(Da-No Ke-Ya)
1903
20 x 15 (50.8 x 38.1)
Private collection

232 Autumn
(Ma-A Sha-Ka)
1903
20 x 15 (50.8 x 38.1)
Unknown

233 Greenie With Jack Rabbit
1903
20 x 15 (50.8 x 38.1)
Unknown

234 Burnham in Red Shirt
1903
7¾ x 5 (19.7 x 12.7)
Unknown

235 None
1904
7 x 5 (17.8 x 12.7)
Unknown

236 Lu & Rosa's Baby
1904
7 x 5 (17.8 x 12.7)
Unknown

237 Warfield Mitchell
1904
7 x 5 (17.8 x 12.7)
Unknown

238 Eva With Greenie
1904
10 x 14 (25.4 x 35.6)
Unknown

239 Nora
1904
15 x 20 (38.1 x 50.8)
Unknown

240 Henry Knight
1904
8 x 6 (20.3 x 15.2)
Unknown

241 Flower Time
(Chi-Do-Mit)
1904
5½ x 7½ (14 x 19.1)
Unknown

242 Isabell
(Carlus' Girl)
1904
5 x 7 (12.7 x 17.8)
Unknown

243 Pawnee Boy
1904
8 x 10 (20.3 x 25.4)
Private collection

244 Lu's Baby Gasky
1904
7 x 5 (17.8 x 12.7)
Unknown

245 Girl Holding Basket
1904
7 x 5 (17.8 x 12.7)
Unknown

246 Ka-We-Si
1904
5¼ x 4¼ (13.3 x 10.8)
Unknown

247 Lark
(Ju-Sil)
1904
10 x 8 (25.4 x 20.3)
Private collection

248 Annie
1904
8 x 6 (20.3 x 15.2)
Unknown

249 Rosa's Baby
1904
7 x 5 (17.8 x 12.7)
Unknown

250 Spring Fever
(Ya'A Tole)
1904
23½ x 17½ (59.7 x 44.5)
Unknown

251 The Adopted
1904
12 x 10 (30.5 x 25.4)
Unknown

252 Rosa's Baby
1904
7 x 5 (17.8 x 12.7)
Unknown

253 Jeff's Daughter
(Mad-Tha-Sway)
1904
20 x 15 (50.8 x 38.1)
Private collection

254 Mollie Dutches' Baby
1904
7 x 5 (17.8 x 12.7)

255 Found In The Brush
1904
23 x 34 (58.4 x 36.4)
Los Angeles Athletic Club

256 Mannie's Child
1904
5 x 7 (12.7 x 17.8)
Private collection

257 Annie
1904
8 x 6 (20.3 x 15.2)
Private collection

258 Thurlow
(Tullo)
1904
6 x 8 (15.2 x 20.3)
Private collection

259 Eva
1904
20 x 15 (50.8 x 38.1)
Unknown

260 Potter Boy Whittle Stick
1904
16 x 14 (40.6 x 35.6)
Private collection

261 Mollie's Baby-Ellen
1904
4½ x 6 (11.4 x 15.2)
Unknown

262 Mollie's Baby Ellen
(Ka-Wi-Lote)
1904
5 x 7 (12.7 x 17.8)
Private collection

263 Rosa Peter's Baby
1905
7 x 5 (17.8 x 12.7)
Private collection

264 Rosita With Young Hare
1905
16 x 24 (40.6 x 61.0)
Private collection

265 Freddie Brigg's Duncan
1905
7 x 5½ (17.8 x 14)
Unknown

266 "Am Coming" Jullo
(Wa-Dum)
1905
7 x 5 (17.8 x 12.7)
Destroyed

267 The River Camp
1905
5 x 7 (12.7 x 17.8)
Unknown

268 Indian Summer
(La-Ha-Min)
1905
20 x 16 (50.8 x 40.6)
Unknown

269 Mollie Wright's Dog
1905
5 x 7 (12.7 x 17.8)
Unknown

270 March
1905
7 x 5 (17.8 x 12.7)
Private collection

271 Thurlow Eating Red Apple
1905
10 x 8 (25.4 x 20.3)
Unknown

272 Daisy's Boy
1905
20 x 16 (50.8 x 40.6)
Unknown

273 Rosie Peter's Girl
1905
7 x 5½ (17.8 x 14)
Unknown

274 Seek The Oracle
1905
16 x 24 (40.6 x 61)
Unknown

275 Child With Rooster
1905
6 x 8 (15.2 x 20.3)
Private collection

276 None
1905
6 x 5½ (15.2 x 14)
Unknown

277 The Comforter
1905
27 x 20 (68.6 x 50.8)
Unknown

278 The Dawning
1905
20 x 16 (50.8 x 40.6)
Unknown

279 Rosita
1905
6 x 10 (15.2 x 25.4)
Unknown

280 Rosa Peter's Baby
1905
6 x 7 (15.2 x 17.8)
Private collection

281 Little Girl
1905
7 x 5 (17.8 x 12.7)
Unknown

282 Baby Ellen
1905
5½ x 5¼ (14 x 13.3)
Unknown

283 Jimmy Knight and Mollie
Wright's Dog
1905
4 x 6¾ (10.2 x 17.2)
Unknown

284 A Bud
(Annie)
1905
10 x 8 (25.4 x 20.3)
Private collection

285 The Sacred Meal
1905
24 x 16 (61 x 40.6)
Private collection

286 None
1905
7 x 5 (17.8 x 12.7)
Unknown

287 Hopland Child
1905
5 x 7 (12.7 x 17.8)
Unknown

288 Garland Mitchell
1905
7 x 5 (17.8 x 12.7)
Destroyed

289 The Dove Garden
1906
17 x 22 (43.2 x 55.9)
Unknown

290 Garland Mitchell
1906
7 x 5 (17.8 x 12.7)
Unknown

291 At My Back Door
1906
8 x 5½ (20.3 x 14)
Private collection

292 None
1906
6½ x 6 (16.5 x 15.2)
Unknown

293 Eba
1906
25 x 18 (63.5 x 45.7)
Unknown

294 Ellen
1906
7 x 5 (17.8 x 12.7)
Private collection

295 Trouble
1906
10 x 14 (25.4 x 35.6)
Unknown

296 Kodina
1906
14½ x 18 (36.8 x 45.7)
Private collection

297 Topsy
1906
9¾ x 12¾ (24.8 x 32.4)
Private collection

298 The Candy Boy
1906
16 x 10½ (40.6 x 26.7)
Unknown

299 Garland Mitchell
1906
7 x 5 (17.8 x 12.7)
Unknown

300 Kelsey Girl
1906
7 x 5 (17.8 x 12.7)
Unknown

301 Ellen
1906
11½ x 5½ (29.2 x 14)
Private collection

302 Petie
1906
8½ x 5 (21.6 x 12.7)
Unknown

303 Garland With Indian Doll
(Pa-Dah)
1906
14½ x 10 (36.8 x 25.4)
Unknown

304 Annie With Apples
1906
13 x 18 (33 x 45.7)
Private collection

305 Joseph–Mary Loff Mitchell's
Baby
1907
7¼ x 5½ (18.4 x 14)
Unknown

306 While Mother Harvests
1907
14 x 11 (35.6 x 27.9)
Unknown

307 "Comrades"
(Ma-Kam)
1907
16 x 12 (40.6 x 30.5)
Private collection

308 A Meddler
(Da-Ko-Him)
1907
7 x 10 (17.8 x 25.4)
Private collection

309 "The Mystic Symbol"
1907
30 x 30 (76.2 x 76.2)
Private collection

310 Tsy
(Blue Jay)
1907
7½ x 5¼ (19.1 x 13.3)
Unknown

311 The Spotted Fawn
1907
16 x 20 (40.6 x 50.8)
Private collection

312 Engaged
(Kay-La-Chin)
1907
25 x 19 (63.5 x 48.3)
Private collection

313 Rosa Peter's William
1907
7 x 5 (17.8 x 12.7)
Unknown

314 Mischief
(Ma-La-Chin)
1907
7½ x 10 (19.1 x 25.4)
Private collection

315 Kill-Dee
(Com-Ti-Di-Li)
1907
5 x 8½ (12.7 x 21.6)
Unknown

316 Warfield Mitchell
1907
12 x 9½ (30.5 x 24.1)
Unknown

317 In Hiding
(E-Nack)
1907
9 x 12 (22.9 x 30.5)
Unknown

318 Flowers
(Pa-Tham)
1907
9½ x 4½ (24.1 x 11.4)
Unknown

319 Spring
(Kat-Sa-mi)
1907
5½ x 8 (14 x 20.3)
Unknown

320 Southwind
(Yo-Ya)
1907
10 x 5 (12.7 x 25.4)
Unknown

321 Whispering Leaves
(Cha-No-Tsi-Tol)
1907
19 x 24 (48.3 x 61)
Unknown

322 William
(Pu-La)
1907
5 x 5 (12.7 x 12.7)
Private collection

323 Sha-Ba Sha-Wy
1907
22 x 15 (55.9 x 38.1)
Unknown

324 Rosa Peter's Baby
1908
6 x 8 (15.2 x 20.3)
Unknown

325 "The Hunters"
1908
18 x 14 (45.7 x 35.6)
Private

326 Rosa Peter's William
     (Nu-Na-Wa)
     8 x 10 (20.3 x 25.4)
     Unknown

327 "Tarweed Gatherer"
     (Ba-Ah Ba-An)
     1908
     20½ x 15 (52 x 38.1)
     Unknown

328 Hudson Mitchell
     1908
     6 x 6 (15.2 x 15.2)
     Unknown

329 Ellen Duncan
     1908
     7 x 5 (17.8 x 12.7)
     Private collection

330 The Little One
     Chuly
     1908
     30 x 36 (76.2 x 91.4)
     Private collection

331 Manchester Boy
     1908
     6½ x 7 (16.5 x 17.8)
     Unknown

332 The Big Brown Owl
     (Na-Ku-Ku)
     1908
     14 x 10½ (35.6 x 26.7)
     Private collection

333 Abalone
     (Da-Wil)
     1908
     14 x 10½ (35.6 x 26.7)
     Private collection

334 Kal-Du-Wit
     1908
     10 x 7 (25.4 x 17.8)
     Private collection

335 The Explorers
     1908
     10 x 6 (25.4 x 15.2)
     Unknown

336 Andrew Williams
     1909
     14 x 10 (35.6 x 25.4)
     Private collection

337 'Trouble
     1909
     20 x 16 (50.8 x 40.6)
     Unknown

338 The Widow
     (Pa-Lol-Chu)
     22 x 17 (55.9 x 43.2)
     Destroyed

339 Rosa Peter's Baby
     1909
     10 x 8 (25.4 x 20.3)
     Private collection

340 John Knight's Boy With
     Long Hair
     1909
     13½ x 10 (34.3 x 25.4)
     Private collection

341 Lake County Girl
     1909
     8½ x 4½ (21.6 x 11.4)
     Unknown

342 Ellen Duncan
     1909
     9 x 4 (22.9 x 10.2)
     Unknown

343 Ja-Kum
     1909
     10 x 5 (25.4 x 12.7)
     Private collection

344 Looking For Trouble
     (Mi-La-Chim)
     1909
     14 x 18 (35.6 x 45.7)
     Private collection

345 Nude Baby
     1909
     6 x 8 (15.2 x 20.3)
     Private collection

346 Boy with Ducklings
     1909
     8 x 10 (20.3 x 25.4)
     Private collection

347 Thom Mitchell Jr.
     1909
     7 x 6 (17.8 x 15.2)
     Unknown

348 Rekis
     1909
     5 x 5½ (12.7 x 14)
     Private collection

349 Angel And William
     1909
     10 x 6 (25.4 x 15.2)
     Unknown

350 A Foolish Young Thing
     (Mi-La-Chim)
     1909
     8½ x 4½ (21.6 x 11.4)
     Private collection

351 Thurlow
1909
10 x 8 (25.4 x 20.3)
Unknown

352 Looking For The Eagle
1909
10 x 5½ (25.4 x 12.7)
Unknown

353 Rosita
1909
14 x 10 (35.6 x 25.4)
Santa Rosa Jr. College

354 Andy
1909
13 x 10 (33 x 25.4)
Private collection

355 A Buffalo Maid
1909
20 x 16 (50.8 x 40.6)
Private collection

356 Annie
1910 – 1911
10 x 5½ (25.4 x 12.7)
Private collection

357 Peter's Baby
1910 – 1911
7 x 5 (17.8 x 12.7)
Private collection

358 Isabel And Thus Jr.
1910 – 1911
10¼ x 5 (26 x 12.7)
Unknown

359 Little Knight Girl
1910 – 1911
9½ x 5 (24.1 x 12.7)
Private collection

360 The Mitty Warrier
1910 – 1911
8 x 4¼ (20.3 x 10.8)
Private collection

361 Wild Flower
(Pu-Tum)
1910 – 1911
10 x 6 (25.4 x 15.2)
Private collection

362 Angel At Work
1910 – 1911
23 x 15 (58.4 x 38.1)
Private collection

363 Mary Christmas Duncan
1910 – 1911
10 x 7 (25.4 x 17.8)
Private collection

364 None
1910 – 1911
7 x 7 (17.8 x 17.8)
Private collection

365 Ellen Duncan
1910 – 1911
10 x 5 (25.4 x 12.7)
Private collection

366 None
1910 – 1911
7 x 4¼ (17.8 x 10.8)
Private collection

367 Child With Rabbit
1910 – 1911
Unknown
Unknown

368 George's Fred's Eva
1910 – 1911
10 x 8 (25.4 x 20.3)
Unknown

369 Thomas Mitchell Jr.
1910 – 1911
7 x 5 (17.8 x 12.7)
Private collection

370 Garland Mitchell
1910 – 1911
14 x 11 (35.6 x 27.9)
Private collection

371 None
1910 – 1911
6½ x 5¼ (16.5 x 13.3)
Private collection

372 The Western Wind
(Bo-Ya)
1910 – 1911
10 x 6 (25.4 x 15.2)
Unknown

373 Matron
(Da-Sho-Ya)
1910 – 1911
23 x 16½ (58.4 x 41.9)
Private collection

374 Basket Maker
1910 – 1911
12 x 12 (30.5 x 30.5)
Unknown

375 Rosa Peter's Baby
1910 – 1911
5¼ x 7 (13.3 x 17.8)
Unknown

376 Clara's Andrew
1910 – 1911
20 x 12 (50.8 x 30.5)
Unknown

377 The Dove Garden
1910 – 1911
23 x 18 (58.4 x 45.7)
Unknown

378 The Basket Maker
1910 – 1911
22 x 18 (55.9 x 45.7)
Private collection

379 Fanny's Girl Grace
1910 - 1911
12 x 8 (30.5 x 20.3)
Unknown

380 Fanny's Infant
1910 – 1911
7 x 5 (17.8 x 12.7)
Unknown

381 Child in Poppie Field
1910 – 1911
10 x 8 (25.4 x 20.3)
Private collection

382 Flower Time
(Chi-Do-Mit)
1910 – 1911
10 x 6 (25.4 x 15.2)
Unknown

383 Lulu Boy, Tom
1910 – 1911
8 x 8 (20.3 x 20.3)
Unknown

384 Little Angel
1910 – 1911
8 x 5 (20.3 x 12.7)
Unknown

385 Fannie's Baby
1910 – 1911
7 x 5 (17.8 x 12.7)
Unknown

386 Ellen Duncan
1910 – 1911
8 x 5½ (20.3 x 14)
Unknown

387 Clara's Baby
1910 – 1911
7 x 5 (17.8 x 12.7)
Unknown

388 Warfield Mitchell
1910 – 1911
7 x 5 (17.8 x 12.7)
Private collection

389 Annie
1910 – 1911
7 x 5 (17.8 x 12.7)
Unknown

390 Mary Christmas Duncan
1910 – 1911
7½ x 4¼ (19.1 x 10.8)
Private collection

391 Garland Mitchell
1910 – 1911
7 x 5 (17.8 x 12.7)
Unknown

392 Ellen Duncan
1910 – 1911
7 x 5 (17.8 x 12.7)
Unknown

393 Ellen Duncan
1910 – 1911
14 x 10 (35.6 x 25.4)
Private collection

394 The Dove
(Ma-Yu)
1910 – 1911
14 x 10¾ (35.6 x 27.3)
Private collection

395 The Crowns Flight
(Ka-ai-Hen)
1910 – 1911
24 x 18 (61 x 45.7)
Private collection

396 Culin Mitchell
1910 – 1911
18 x 14 (45.7 x 35.6)
Private collection

397 Ellen Duncan
1910 – 1911
14 x 10 (35.6 x 25.4)
Unknown

398 Pomo Child
1910 – 1911
10 x 14 (25.4 x 35.6)
Unknown

399 Pomo Infant
1910 – 1911
14 x 10 (35.6 x 25.4)
Unknown

400 Little Girl
1911
8½ x 5 (21.6 x 12.7)
Unknown

401 None
1911
14 x 10 (35.6 x 25.4)
Private collection

402 Ho-y
1911
7 x 5 (17.8 x 12.7)
Private collection

403 Ellen Duncan
1912
11 x 8 (27.9 x 20.3)
Private collection

404 Poma Basket Maker
1912
15 x 20 (38.1 x 50.8)
Private collection

405 Lily
(Ka-Shi-Lau)
1912
24 x 18 (61 x 45.7)
Private collection

406 The Bear Woman
1912
24 x 20 (61 x 50.8)
Private collection

407 Portrait of a Pomo Chief
1912
20 x 15 (50.8 x 38.1)
Private collection

408 Kay-Will
1912
20 x 16 (50.8 x 40.6)
Shasta State Historical
Society

409 "The Lark"
(Ju-Shil)
1912
24 x 18 (61 x 45.7)
Private collection

410 None
1912
14 x 10 (35.6 x 25.4)
Unknown

411 Kay-Will
1912
20 x 16 (50.8 x 40.6)
Private collection

412 Indian Dancer
1912
20 x 16 (50.8 x 40.6)
Private collection

413 Joseph Mitchell
1912
14 x 10 (35.6 x 25.4)
Private collection

414 Poma Medicine Man
1912
24 x 18 (61 x 45.7)
Private collection

415 The First Lesson
(Rosa James Girl)
1912
18 x 12 (45.7 x 30.5)
Unknown

416 Kay-Will
1912
20 x 16 (50.8 x 40.6)
Private collection

417 Little Brothers
1912
6 x 10 (15.2 x 25.4)
Unknown

418 Warfield Mitchell
(Gol-Mul)
1912
14 x 10 (35.6 x 25.4)
Unknown

419 William Mitchell
(Col-Lip-Win)
1912
18 x 12 (45.7 x 30.5)
Private collection

420 Little Woman
(Mad-Tha-Koo)
1912
15 x 11 (38.1 x 27.9)
Private collection

421 Thomas Mitchell Jr.
(Little Ja-Kum)
1912
14 x 10 (35.6 x 25.4)
Unknown

422 Friend or Foe
(Tracks)
1912
22 x 18 (55.9 x 45.7)
Unknown

423 "Rosita"
1912
22 x 15 (55.9 x 38.1)
Unknown

424 A Little Flower
("Po-Thum")
1912
14 x 10 (35.6 x 25.4)
Private collection

425 Kay-Will
(Fur Cape-Pipe-Bandana)
1912
20 x 15 (50.8 x 38.1)
Unknown

426 "The Only One"
(Ul-Dool)
1913
14 x 10 (35.6 x 25.4)
Unknown

427 Portrait of Poma Matron
1913
20 x 16 (50.8 x 40.6)
Unknown

428 Molly Wright's Niece
1913
18 x 13 (45.7 x 33)
Unknown

429 Ma-Yu
1913
14 x 10 (35.6 x 25.4)
Private collection

430 The Little Rabbit
(Ma-Ku)
1913
14 x 10 (35.6 x 25.4)
Unknown

431 "Ka-Dai"
1913
22 x 16 (55.9 x 40.6)
Private collection

432 Bashful
(Meet-Sune)
1913
16 x 12 (40.6 x 30.5)
Unknown

433 Old Mary Pinto
(Ka-Wi-A)
1913
22 x 16 (55.9 x 40.6)
Private collection

434 None
1913
16 x 12 (40.6 x 30.5)
Unknown

435 The Feast Gift
(Lol-Di-Tut)
1913
24 x 18 (61 x 45.7)
Unknown

436 Ellen Duncan
1913
12 x 9 (30.5 x 22.9)
Private collection

437 "The Call Of Makila
Mad-Tha"
1913
28 x 22 (71.1 x 55.9)
Unknown

438 Andrew With Orange
1913
16 x 12 (40.6 x 30.5)
Private collection

439 "The Talking Fawn"
1913
20 x 16 (50.8 x 40.6)
Private collection

440 None
1913
16 x 12 (40.6 x 30.5)
Private collection

441 Garland Mitchell
1913
14 x 10 (35.6 x 25.4)
Unknown

442 None
1913
20 x 16 (50.8 x 40.6)
Unknown

443 The Last Stitch
(Tul-E-Ba)
16 x 22 (40.6 x 55.9)
Private collection

444 "The Knight Baby"
1913
14 x 10 (35.6 x 25.4)
Unknown

445 Fitch
1913
14 x 10 (35.6 x 25.4)
Unknown

446 Ta-Le-A And Padah
1913
22 x 16 (55.9 x 40.6)
Unknown

447 The Tar-Maid
(Ba-One Na-Ko-Sa)
1913
24 x 18 (61 x 45.7)
Unknown

448 "The Pilferer"
(Ma-Ka)
1914
22 x 16 (55.9 x 40.6)
Private collection

449 Poma Children
1914
20 x 16 (50.8 x 40.6)
Unknown

450 Clover Time
(Tso-Ma)
1914
26 x 18 (66 x 45.7)
Unknown

451 He Loves You or "The
     Song Of The Lark"
     (Jushle)
     1914
     26 x 18 (66 x 45.7)
     Unknown

452 "The Lonesome Hour"
     1914
     28¼ x 21¾ (71.8 x 55.2)
     Private collection

453 None
     1914
     22 x 16 (55.9 x 40.6)
     Unknown

454 None
     1914
     20 x 16 (50.8 x 40.6)
     Private collection

455 Peace
     (Ho-Mu)
     1914
     19½ 27½ (49.5 x 69.9)
     Private collection

456 The Charmer of Flowers
     1914
     22 x 16 (55.9 x 40.6)
     Private collection

457 Garland Mitchell
     1914
     20 x 16 (50.8 x 40.6)
     Unknown

458 Poma Basket Maker
     1914
     22 x 16 (55.9 x 40.6)
     Unknown

459 "The Watermelon"
     1914
     24 x 30 (61 x 76.2)
     Private collection

460 "The Pick of the Patch"
     1914
     16 x 20 (40.6 x 50.8)
     Unknown

461 The Coming of
     Ma-ki-la Mad-tha
     1914
     24 x 18 (61 x 45.7)
     Private collection

462 Natives
     (Ski-Ko-Da)
     1914
     20 x 16 (50.8 x 40.6)
     Private collection

463 "We Got Him"
     1914
     20 x 16 (50.8 x 40.6)
     Private collection

464 The Wedding Guest
     (Ov-Ne)
     1914
     24 x 18 (61 x 45.7)
     Private collection

465 "Tale-O and Squirrels"
     1914
     20 x 16 (50.8 x 40.6)
     Private collection

466 The Big Brown Owl
     (Ma-Ku-Ku)
     1914
     24 x 18 (61 x 45.7)
     Private collection

467 A Sportsman
     (Kol-Pa)
     1914
     20 x 16 (50.8 x 40.6)
     Private collection

468 Woodpecker
     (Ka-Totch)
     1914
     24 x 18 (61 x 45.7)
     Private collection

469 Head of Huxon
     1914
     14 x 10 (35.6 x 25.4)
     Private collection

470 Hunting Tsy
     (Blue Jay)
     1914
     24 x 18 (61 x 45.7)
     Private collection

471 Culin Mitchell
     1914
     20 x 16 (50.8 x 40.6)
     Private collection

472 Willum and Chuly
     1914
     16 x 20 (40.6 x 50.8)
     Unknown

473 A Hunter
     (Teck-E-Dy)
     1914
     Unknown
     Private collection

474 Kay-Wil Lighting His Pipe
     1914
     22 x 16 (55.9 x 40.6)
     Private collection

475 The Wild Pidgeon
     (Chi-Bot-Ba)
     1914
     18 x 12 (45.7 x 30.5)
     Private collection

476 Botler Flies (Qui-Tak-Tak)
1914
24 x 18 (61 x 45.7)
Private collection

477 Hark The Squirrel
(Sho-Ma-Ma Begay!)
1916
20 x 16 (50.8 x 40.6)
Private collection

478 The War Eagle
(Shai)
1916
27 x 20 (68.6 x 50.8)
Private collection

479 Little Jack
1916
21½ x 12½ (54.6 x 31.8)
Private collection

480 Mountain Spirit
(Da-No-Cha)
1914
22 x 16 (55.9 x 40.6)
Unknown

481 Savages
1916
12 x 10 (30.5 x 25.4)
Private collection

482 Little Brother
(Ma-Ti-Ga)
1916
10¼ x 5¼ (26 x 13.3)
Private collection

483 The "Prayer Baby"
1916
14 x 10 (35.6 x 25.4)
Private collection

484 The Passing Of Makila-Madtha
1916
24 x 18 (61 x 45.7)
Private collection

485 The Sunny Side
1916
10 x 12 (25.4 x 30.5)
Unknown

486 Ta-Le-A
1916
16 x 12 (40.6 x 30.5)
Unknown

487 The Pidgeon Told
(Sho-Pinny)
1916
20 x 15 (50.8 x 38.1)
Private collection

488 A Christening
1916
22 x 16 (55.9 x 40.6)
Private collection

489 Clover Blossom
(Tso-Pot-Thum)
1916
14 x 10 (35.6 x 25.4)
Private collection

490 A Quail
1916
18 x 12 (45.7 x 30.5)
Private collection

491 A Hunter
(Tick-E-Dy)
1916
22 x 16 (55.9 x 40.6)
Private collection

492 The Dove Place
(Ma-Yu-Ma)
1914
24 x 19 (61 x 48.3)
Private collection

493 Culin Mitchell and Shaili
1914
20 x 16 (50.8 x 40.6)
Private collection

494 White Person
(Ma-San)
1916
12 x 10 (30.5 x 25.4)
Private collection

495 The Chipmunk
(Ba-Tsim-Tsi)
1917
16 x 20 (40.6 x 50.8)
Private collection

496 The Orphan
(Chu-Bomi)
1917
19½ x 13½ (49.5 x 34.3)
Private collection

497 Mermaid
(Plite-Li-Us)
1917
14 x 10 (35.6 x 25.4)
Unknown

498 Ray Of Light
(Da-Ta-Leu)
1917
16 x 10 (40.6 x 25.4)
Private collection

499 Gimini
1917
16 x 13½ (40.6 x 34.3)
Private collection

500 Wayside Flower
(Kal-Si)
1917
23 x 13 (58.4 x 33)
Private collection

501 Ka-Wi-Lote
July 3, 1917
14 x 10 (35.6 x 25.4)
Private collection

502 "A Hold Up"
August 20, 1917
20 x 17 (50.8 x 43.2)
Private collection

503 "A Piaute Venus"
September 26, 1917
25 x 14 (63.5 x 35.6)
Private collection

504 Helen
September 26, 1917
16 x 11 (40.6 x 27.9)
Private collection

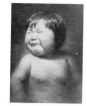

505 "Ruler Of The House"
(Cha-Ka-Li)
December 18, 1917
14 x 10 (35.6 x 25.4)
Private collection

506 "Wild Roses"
(Ba-Ka-Ka)
March 3, 1918
16 x 10½ (40.6 x 26.7)
Private collection

507 A Summer Day
April 30, 1918
20 x 16 (50.8 x 40.6)
Private collection

508 "The Brush Hut Baby"
(Shah Ka-Wi-A)—Annie
May 13, 1918
14 x 10 (35.6 x 25.4)
Private collection

509 "New Clam Shell"
(Kal-Na-Sway)
June 5, 1918
22 x 16 (55.9 x 40.6)
Private collection

510 The Daughter Of The Quail
Woman
September 12, 1918
22 x 16 (55.9 x 40.6)
Private collection

511 Oracle Of The Leaves
August 14, 1918
24½ x 20 (62.2 x 50.8)
Private collection

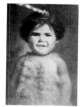

512 Andy
(Tsu-Li-Bu)
September 5, 1918
16 x 12 (40.6 x 30.5)
Private collection

513 Star Eyes
(To-Tol-Ovi)
October 14, 1918
20 x 16 (50.8 x 40.6)
Private collection

514 "The Other One"
(Du-Ko-Li)
November 26, 1918
14 x 10 (35.6 x 25.4)
Private collection

515 "A Work"
(Wip-Um)
November 26, 1918
17 x 12 (43.2 x 30.5)
Private collection

516 Little Brothers
(Ma-Ti-Ga)
November 16, 1918
20 x 16 (50.8 x 40.6)
Private collection

517 "The Rain Woman"
(Ma-Ki-La Mad-Tha)
December 18, 1918
20 x 15 (50.8 x 38.1)
Private collection

518 Fatty
(Pu-I)
December 1918
14 x 10 (35.6 x 25.4)
Private collection

519 Lena's Baby
(Le-Na-Wi)
December 1918
14 x 10 (35.6 x 25.4)
Unknown

520 Jack Rabbit
(Shi-Ko-Da)
January 1918
22½ x 14 (57.2 x 35.6)
Unknown

521 Just Wait Until We Get
To A Good Place
1919
20 x 16 (50.8 x 40.6)
Museum of Art, Cleveland, Ohio

522 "A Little Savage"
1919
14 x 10 (35.6 x 25.4)
Private collection

523 Kol-Ba And The Yellow One
(Kolba and Hai-Yu
Cha-Bot)
1919
20 x 16 (50.8 x 40.6)
Private collection

524 The Adventurers
1919
20 x 16 (50.8 x 40.6)
Private collection

525 Hu-Hi-Ya and Bu-Shay
1919
20 x 16 (50.8 x 40.6)
Private collection

526 Off The Highway
1919
16 x 10 (40.6 x 25.4)
Private collection

527 Pinole For The Dead
1919
25 x 20 (63.5 x 40.6)
Private collection

528 "A Gift"
(Ko-Di-Man)
1919
14 x 10 (35.6 x 25.4)
Private collection

529 Big Fish
(Yo-Shu)
1919
20 x 16 (50.8 x 40.6)
Private collection

530 Wul-A-By With Orange
1919
16 x 12 (40.6 x 30.5)
Private collection

531 Scharf And Chuddy
1919
20 x 16 (50.8 x 40.6)
Unknown

532 Little Young Rabbit
(Shi-Bo-Da Ho-y)
1919
20 x 15 (50.8 x 38.1)
Private collection

533 "The Foxes"
(Koli-pi-ta)
1919
24 x 18 (61 x 45.7)
Private collection

534 "Looks Like A Shell"
(Kol-Pi-Ta)
1919
14 x 10 (35.6 x 25.4)
Unknown

535 Tribal Singer
(Ka-Me-Ya)
1919
20 x 14 (50.8 x 35.6)
Private collection

536 The Rain Doll
(Shaili)
1920
21 x 16 (53.3 x 40.6)
Unknown

537 "Our Home"
(Yath Chow)
1920
16 x 22 (40.6 x 55.9)
Private collection

538 Culin And Shaili
1920
20 x 16 (50.8 x 40.6)
Private collection

539 Surf Fish
(Chu Shuw)
1920
16 x 22 (40.6 x 55.9)
Private collection

540 Bear Woman
(Buta-Madtha)
1920
26 x 20 (66 x 50.8)
Private collection

541 Tear Baby
(U-I-Ka)
1921
14 x 10 (35.6 x 25.4)
Private collection

542 A Wonderful Thing
(Tsim)
1921
16 x 20 (40.6 x 50.8)
Private collection

543 Eyes Of The West
(Oui-Bo)
1921
16 x 12 (40.6 x 30.5)
Unknown

544 Fear Of A Hat
(Som-Le-Ti-Tsaka)
1921
20 x 16 (50.8 x 40.6)
Unknown

545 Wid-On And The Poppies
1921
20 x 13 (50.8 x 33)
Unknown

546 Molly And Child
1921
24 x 20 (61 x 50.8)
Private collection

547 "Bet I Get Him"
1921
20 x 16 (50.8 x 40.6)
Unknown

548 Stranger Baby
(Ya-Cha Ka-Wy)
1921
14 x 10 (35.6 x 25.4)
Private collection

549 Young Basket Maker
1921
16 x 10 (40.6 x 25.4)
Private collection

550 War-Fel
1921
16 x 12 (40.6 x 30.5)
Private collection

551 Border Land
1922
16 x 20 (40.6 x 50.8)
Private collection

552 Greenie
(Kats-Am)
1922
16 x 10 (40.6 x 25.4)
Unknown

553 Kol-Pa
1922
14 x 10 (35.6 x 25.4)
Private collection

554 Ka-Tat
1922
16 x 11 (40.6 x 27.9)
Private collection

555 Kol-Pa
1922
14 x 10 (35.6 x 25.4)
Private collection

556 Culin Mitchell
1922
16 x 10 (40.6 x 25.4)
Private collection

557 The Orphan
(Chu-Bome)
1922
16 x 10 (40.6 x 25.4)
Private collection

558 Leaves Talking
(Tsi-Tol Cha-None)
1922
14½ x 10½ (36.8 x 26.7)
Private collection

559 Annie's Helen
1922
16 x 10 (40.6 x 25.4)
Unknown

560 "The Bethrothed"
(Ta-Le-A)
1922
22 x 16 (55.9 x 40.6)
Private collection

561 "The Grandchildren"
1922
20 x 16 (50.8 x 40.6)
Private collection

562 Mollie Duncan's Robba
1922
14 x 10 (35.6 x 25.4)
Private collection

563 Hudson Mitchell
1922
14 x 10 (35.6 x 25.4)
Unknown

564 Shaili And Fox
(Chi-Yah-Li)
1922
20 x 16 (50.8 x 40.6)
Unknown

565 Young Girl Dancer
(Ma-Tu-Tsi Ka-Wy)
1922
16 x 10 (40.6 x 25.4)
Unknown

566 "The New Baby"
(Ku-La-Ka)
1923
16 x 20 (40.6 x 50.8)
Private collection

567 New Woman
(Mad-Tha Sway)
1923
16 x 10 (40.6 x 25.4)
Unknown

568 Bush Baby
(Si-Ek-Late)
1923
16 x 10 (40.6 x 25.4)
Private collection

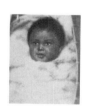

569 Mu-La-Hi
1923
14 x 10 (35.6 x 25.4)
Private collection

570 Going Fishing
1923
20 x 16 (50.8 x 40.6)
Private collection

571 Ta-Le-A And Shi-Ko-Do
1923
23 x 17 (58.4 x 43.2)
Private collection

572 Ellen Moore
1923
16 x 11 (40.6 x 27.9)
Private collection

573 Clement
1923
16 x 10 (40.6 x 25.4)
Unknown

574 Sish-Ma
1923
16 x 10 (40.6 x 25.4)
Private collection

575 A Hop Picker
(Culin)
1923
16 x 10 (40.6 x 25.4)
Private collection

576 Annie
(Shaili)
1923
14 x 10 (35.6 x 25.4)
Private collection

577 The Big Kill
1923
17 x 14 (43.2 x 35.6)
Private collection

578 "Harvesters"
1923
17 x 14 (43.2 x 35.6)
Private collection

579 Mollie Duncan's Robba
(Oui-Bo)
1923
14 x 10 (35.6 x 25.4)
Private collection

580 When The Birds Went
To War
(Kal-Pin)
1923
Unknown
Unknown

581 "The Basket Maker"
(Mary Luff Mitchell)
1923
12 x 16 (30.5 x 40.6)
Private collection

582 The Great Spirit
1924
24 x 18 (61 x 45.7)
Private collection

583 "Butter Flies"
(Le-La-Wa)
1924
25 x 20 (63.5 x 40.6)
Private collection

584 By The Great Highway
(Robba)
1924
10 x 14 (25.4 x 35.6)
Private collection

585 Francis
(Pran-Sa)
1924
16 x 10 (40.6 x 25.4)
Unknown

588 Sea Shore
(Ka-Ma-Lel)
1924
14 x 10 (35.6 x 25.4)
Unknown

586 Oui-Bo And Shef
1924
18 x 12 (45.7 x 30.5)
Private collection

587 No Name
(Ba-Shi-Shom)
1924
14 x 10 (35.6 x 25.4)
Private collection

589 "The Butterfly"
(Le-La-Wa)
1924
10 x 14 (25.4 x 35.6)
Private collection

590 Rosa, The First Convert
1924
27½ x 25½ (69.9 x 64.8)
Private collection

591 "What The Puppy Did"
1924
14 x 10 (35.6 x 25.4)
Unknown

592 Du-Wy
1924
16 x 12 (40.6 x 30.5)
Private collection

593 The Grand Mother
(Ba-Dai)
1924
26 x 20 (66 x 50.8)
Private collection

594 Wild Roses
(Ka-Ba-Ka)
1925
17 x 11 (43.2 x 27.9)
Unknown

595 Innocence
1925
22 x 16 (55.9 x 40.6)
Private collection

596 Ellen Duncan
1925
16 x 10 (40.6 x 25.4)
Private collection

597 Highway Flowers
1925
14 x 10 (35.6 x 25.4)
Private collection

598 The Good Old Summer Time
1925
17 x 11 (43.2 x 27.9)
Private collection

599 Quail Baby
(Chi-Ka-Ka)
1925
14 x 10 (35.6 x 25.4)
Private collection

600 Mountain Lilac
(Ba-Kam Se-Dote)
1925
12 x 10 (30.5 x 25.4)
Private collection

601 Kati-Brin And Ka-Tum
1921
16 x 12 (40.6 x 30.5)
Private collection

602 A Hereditary Chief
(Ta-Ta (The Hawk))
1926
16 x 10 (40.6 x 25.4)
Private collection

603 Western Wilds
(Kol-Pi-Ta)
1926
16½ x 12 (419 x 30.5)
Private collection

604 Going To Grandma's
Kal-Tai (Winner Of Wampum)
1926
16½ x 12 (419 x 30.5)
Private collection

605 Let The Nation Worry
Tsa-Tu (Green Things)
1926
20 x 16 (50.8 x 40.6)
Private collection

606 Love's Messenger
1926
21 x 17 (53.3 x 43.2)
Private collection

607 Let Others Worry
1927
21 x 17 (53.3 x 43.2)
Private collection

608 The Dove
(Ma-Yu)
1927
16 x 12 (40.6 x 30.5)
Private collection

609 Eyes Of The West
1927
16 x 12 (40.6 x 30.5)
Private collection

610 Ma-Yu
1927
16 x 12 (40.6 x 30.5)
Private collection

611 Western Wild Flowers
(Hu-Hi-A And Chi-Koda)
1927
15 x 10 (38.1 x 25.4)
Private collection

612 The Betrothed
(Da-Han Shu-Way)
1927
22 x 16 (55.9 x 40.6)
Unknown

613 Left Behind
(Kol-Piu)
1927
14 x 10 (35.6 x 25.4)
Private collection

614 Primitives
(Be-Tune)
1927
18 x 20 (45.7 x 50.8)
Private collection

615 Ellen
(Kay-Ta-Na)
1927
10 x 15 (25.4 x 38.1)
Private collection

616 Little Brothers
(Li-Nu-Ky)
1927
20 x 16 (50.8 x 40.6)
Private collection

617 Without Fault
(Shot-Das)
1927
16 x 12 (40.6 x 30.5)
Private collection

618 Ellen Duncan
(Oui-Tak-Tak)
1927
14 x 10 (35.6 x 25.4)
Unknown

619 Helen
(Oui-Tak-Tak Kol-Di-Le)
1927
10 x 14 (25.4 x 35.6)
Private collection

620 Betume
1927
16 x 12 (40.6 x 30.5)
Unknown

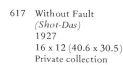

621 Culin
(Kal-Na-Mi)
1927
16 x 12 (40.6 x 30.5)
Private collection

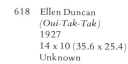

622 Our Little Brothers
1928
20½ x 15½ (52.0 x 39.4)
Private collection

623 Betume
1928
16 x 22 (40.6 x 55.9)
Private collection

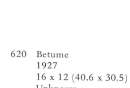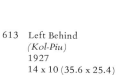

624 The Day We Eat
(Kol-Pin And She-Dote)
1928
20 x 16 (50.8 x 40.6)
Unknown

625 The Betrothed
(Da-Hi-Da)
1928
22 x 16 (55.9 x 40.6)
Private collection

626 Wild Roses
1928
22 x 16 (55.9 x 40.6)
Private collection

627 Be-Tume
1928
17 x 12 (43.2 x 30.5)
Private collection

628 The Peaceful Pipe
(Kal-Ba)
1928
24 x 16 (61 x 40.6)
Private collection

629 The Sacred Meal
1928
24 x 16 (61 x 40.6)
Unknown

630 The Story Teller
1927
20 x 16 (50.8 x 40.6)
Private collection

631 Light Flies
(Da-Chow)
1928
14 x 10 (35.6 x 25.4)
Private collection

632 Old John Scott
1928
20 x 16 (50.8 x 40.6)
Private collection

633 Girl's Head
(Ka-Ta-Li)
1928
14 x 10 (35.6 x 25.4)
Private collection

634 Robba
1928
16 x 10 (40.6 x 25.4)
Private collection

635 When The Birds Went
To War
(Kal-Pui)
1928
20 x 16 (50.8 x 40.6)
Private collection

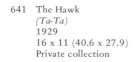

636 The Grandmother
(Ba-Dai)
1928
20 x 16 (50.8 x 40.6)
Private collection

637 Kay Will
1928
20 x 16 (50.8 x 40.6)
Private collection

638 The Little Rabbit
(Mi-Kyu)
1928
14 x 10 (35.6 x 25.4)
Private collection

639 Mary Pinto
(Ka-Mi-D)
1928
20 x 16 (50.8 x 40.6)
Private collection

640 Baby Ellen
1929
16 x 10 (40.6 x 25.4)
Private collection

641 The Hawk
(Ta-Ta)
1929
16 x 11 (40.6 x 27.9)
Private collection

642 The Angel Of The Lodge
(Ta-Ta)
1929
16 x 11 (40.6 x 27.9)
Unknown

643 Little Teck-E-Dy
1929
14 x 10 (35.6 x 25.4)
Private collection

644 Weeds & Flowers
1929
16 x 10 (40.6 x 25.4)
Unknown

645 The Singing Throat
(The Ki-Me-Ya)
1929
26 x 20 (66 x 50.8)
Private collection

646 The Rain Doll
(Ma-Dim)
1930
16 x 10 (40.6 x 25.4)
Private collection

647 The Bride
1930
24½ x 20 (62.2 x 50.8)
Private collection

648 Basket Baby
1930
14 x 10 (35.6 x 25.4)
Unknown

649 Basket Baby & Dog
1930
14 x 10 (35.6 x 25.4)
Private collection

650 The Quail Baby
(Ta-Lera And Betune)
1930
22 x 16 (55.9 x 40.6)
Private collection

651   The Butterfly
(Oui-Tak-Tak)
1931
16 x 12 (40.6 x 30.5)
Private collection

652   It Is A Good World
(Betoom)
1931
16 x 12 (40.6 x 30.5)
Private collection

653   Pomo Indian Boy
1932
20 x 16 (50.8 x 40.6)
Private collection

654   Bill
1932
16 x 12 (40.6 x 30.5)
Private collection

655   Head Of Pomo Indian Child
1932
16 x 12 (40.6 x 30.5)
Private collection

656   The Dawn Of Song
(La-Mu) (Gopher Man)
1932
20½ x 26½ (52.0 x 67.3)
Ukiah Public Library

657   Yesterday
(Kol-Ba)
1933
24 x 14 (61 x 35.6)
Private collection

658   Kay-Will With Cane
1933
24 x 14 (61 x 35.6)
Private collection

659   The Wedding Guest
1933
16½ x 32 (41.9 x 81.3)
Private collection

660   Eagle Chief
1933
24 x 14 (61 x 35.6)
Private collection

661   Eagle Chief
1933
24 x 14 (61 x 35.6)
Private collection

662   Te-Ha-Ra
1933
24 x 14 (61 x 35.6)
Private collection

663   Joseypa
1933
22 x 16 (55.9 x 40.6)
Private collection

664   When The Birds Went
To War
1933
18 x 10 (45.7 x 25.4)
Private collection

665   Baby Head Yawning
(Kol-Si) (The Distant One)
1933
16 x 10 (40.6 x 25.4)
Private collection

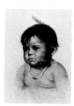

666   Baby Head
1933
14 x 10 (35.6 x 25.4)
Private collection

667   Ka-Ba-Ka)
1933
18 x 10 (45.7 x 25.4)
Private collection

668   Head of Betoon
1933
18 x 10 (45.7 x 25.4)
Unknown

669   Basket Baby
(Tsin-Ta-Na)
1933
16 x 12 (40.6 x 30.5)
Private collection

670   The Dowry
1933
17 x 32 (43.2 x 81.3)
Private collection

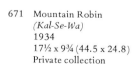

671   Mountain Robin
(Kal-Se-Wa)
1934
17½ x 9¾ (44.5 x 24.8)
Private collection

672   Boy With Fish Pole
1933
20 x 10 (50.8 x 25.4)
Private collection

673   Basket Boy
1933
18 x 10 (45.7 x 25.4)
Private collection

674   Basket Baby
(Ket-Bim)
1933
13 x 18½ (33 x 21.6)
Private collection

675   Old Tom Jamison
1933
18 x 10 (25.4 x 45.7)
Unknown

676 Cha-Bok And Kay-Kay-Pun
1934
18 x 24 (45.7 x 61)
Private collection

677 Pomo Indian Boy
1934
16 x 12 (40.6 x 30.5)
Private collection

678 Topsy
(*Kol-Pi-Ta*)
1934
35 x 18 (88.9 x 45.7)
Unknown

679 Pomo Indian Child
1935
25 x 13 (63.5 x 33)
Private collection

680 Basket Baby
(*Ho-wy*)
1935
16 x 10 (40.6 x 25.4)
Private collection

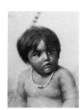

681 Boy With Watermelon
1935
16 x 12 (40.6 x 30.5)
Private collection

682 Andy
1935
16 x 10 (40.6 x 25.4)
Private collection

683 The Dove
(*Ma-Yu*)
1935
18 x 10 (45.7 x 25.4)
Private collection

684 Basket Baby
1935
18 x 10 (45.7 x 25.4)
Private collection

INDEX

A Kamaaina 58
Adventurers, The [524] 79
Am Coming Jullo (Wa-Dum) [266] 65
Among the Poppies 66
Andy with a Cut Finger [49] 42
Annie [161] 65
Apple Baby [19] 34

Ba-ka-kai [506] 70
Baby, The [70] 44
Baby Bunting [24] 35
Baby Fitch [79] 46
Basket Baby [684] 90, 156
Basket Maker, The [378] 117
Basket Maker, The [581] 154
Basket Picnic 66
Bear Woman, The (Bu-ta Mad-tha) [406] 73, 74
Belle of the Tribe (Katum) [2] 27, 28, 32
Betrothed, The (Ta-Le-A) [560] 138
Betrothed, The [612] 88
Billy Kept Plump [15] 32
Blue Monday [66] 42
Boss, The (Kay Kah-wy) [63] 98
Boy with Ducklings [346] 113
Boy with Watermelon [681] 90, 155
Bride, The [647] 88, 149
Buffalo Maid, A [355] 69

Call of Makila Mad-tha, The [437] 74
Calling of the Kiota (God), The 50
Candy Boy, The [298] 66
Captain John [3] 28, 55
Cha-bok and Kay-kay-pun [676] 153
Chi-bot-ta see The Wild Pigeon
Child with Rabbit [367] 70
Children with a Bird's Nest [601] 87
Chinese Girl Laughing [188] 108
Chipmunk, The (Ba-tsim-tsi) [495] 127
Chuly see The Little One
Col-lip-win [419] 75, 120
Comforter, The [277] 110
Coming of the Coyote [109] 50
Cornered 47
Crows Flight, The [395] 74
Crying Baby 55
Culin and Shaili [538] 80, 84
Culin Mitchell [396] 79, 80, 81
Culin Mitchell [471] 79, 80
Culin Mitchell and Shaili [493] 80

Dancer, The [136] 43
Dawn of Song, The (La-mu) (Gopher Man) [656] 148
Di-hi-da [625] 88
Diplomat, The [162] 53
Disappointment [21] 34
Do-Sho-Ya [373] 74

Dove, The (Ma-yu) [683] 90
Dove Garden, The [289] 66
Dove Garden, The [377] 74
Dove Place, The (Ma-yu-ma) [492] 66, 124
Dowry, The [212] 58, 88, 110
Du-ko-li see The Other One

E-nach 67
Eagle Chief [660] [661] 88, 89
Early Birds [30] 38
Empty Basket, The [81] 50, 101
Engaged 67
Eyes of the Highway [609] 142

First Jack, The [84] 103
First Lesson, The [415] 70
First Pang, The [41] 38, 42
Found in the Brush [255] 112
Foxes, The [533] 80, 140
Friends see Lonesome

Garland Mitchell [288] 65
Gimini [499] 130
Good Old Summer Time [598] 147
Grace Carpenter [92] 43
Grandchildren, The [561] 141
Greenie [62] [77] 44
Greenie (Kats-am) [552] 85
Greenie with Two Yellow Puppies [73] 44

Hard Times see Who Comes
Hard Times 36
Hark that Squirrel (Sho-ma-ma begay) [477] 125
Hawaiian Girl [186] 107
Hawaiian Woman [190] 65
He Loves You [451] 78
Head of John Jake's Father (Kol-Ba) [177] 105
Helen (Qui-tak-tak Kol-di-le) [619] 142
Help on the Dow [114] 102
Hilo Girl [211] 65
Ho-y 67
Hogs [99] 51
Hold Up, A [502] 133
Holy Mary [636] 151
Home Care (Myrt) [172] 54, 104
Hop Picker, The (Culin) [575] 81
Hu-hi-ya and Bu-shay [525] 77, 133
Hunters, The [325] 69

Indian Child with Fawn [439] 77
Indian Dancer [412] 75
Indian Summer (La-Ha-Min) [268] 111
Interrupted Bath, The (Quail Baby) [4] 29, 30, 32
It is a Good World (Betoom) [652] 145

Jimmie 40

Ka-wi-lote [501] 81, 82
Kal-si see Wayside Flowers
Kay-will see Portrait of a Poma Chief
Kay-will [637] 150
Knights of the Forest [82] 65
Kol-pa [553] 65

Lark, The (Ju-Shil) [409] 74
Leaves Talking (Tsi-tol Cha-none) [558] 85
Left Behind (Kol-piu) [613] 144
Lei Girl [187] 109
Let's Make Up [78] 49
Little Brothers [417] 70
Little Girl in Poppie Field [381] 119
Little Jack [479] 128
Little Mendocino [5] 29, 30, 31, 32, 51, 55, 93
Little One, The (Chuly) [330] 69, 114
Little Piper, The [34] 42
Little Savage, A [522] 83
Little Woman (Mad-tha-koo) [420] 120
Lonesome (Friends) [18] 34
Lonesome Hour, The [452] 78, 121

Ma-ka (The Pilferer) [448] 118
Mad-tha-koo see Little Woman
Mad-tha-koo [420] 75, 76
Mamma [29] 36, 37, 55, 65
Mary Angel [504] 82
Mary Low Eating Poi (A Kamaaina) [196] 57, 107
May Carpenter Ellis [56] 43
Mendocino Products [45] 42
Mity Warrier [360] 69
Mollie see Powley's Sweetheart
My Name-sake [33] 97
Mystic Symbol, The [309] 68, 115

National Thorn [1] 25, 26, 27, 29, 32, 39, 42
Natives [462] 79

Old Couple (Ko-Di-Na) [139] 65
Old Hawaiian Woman [209] 108
Oracle of the Leaves, The [511] 132
Orphan, The [113] 50, 51, 68, 101
Other One, The (Du-ko-li) [514] 136
Our Home (Yath Chow) [537] 134

Pa-dah 67
Pa-tham 67
Passing of Ma-ki-la Mad-tha, The [484] 79
Pete McClure and Mollie Duncan [676] 89, 90
Piaute Venus, A [503] 135
Pilferer, The see Ma-ka
Pinole for the Dead [527] 83
Plotters, The see The Foxes
Plotters, The 80
Poma Basket Maker [404] 74
Poma Children and a Dog in the Rain [461] 79, 125
Poma Medicine Man [414] 76
Pomo Child with Dog [442] 77
Pomo Indian Baby with Apple [434] 77
Pomo Indian Children in Ma-tu Woods [440] 77
Portrait of a Poma Chief [407] 74, 116
Portrait of a Poma Chief [408] 74
Powley [43] 99
Powley's Sweetheart [40] 41
Primatives [614] 87
Punahele 58

Quail Baby see The Interrupted Bath
Quail Hunter, The [69] 45, 46, 65

Rain Doll, The (Shaili) [536] 146
Rain Woman, The [517] 79
Ray of Light (Da-Ta-Leu) [498] 131
Rosa, The First Convert [590] 139
Rosie [36] 44
Runaway, The [72] 46, 48

Seed Conjurer, The [61] 43, 100
Shaili Mitchell [493] 80
Song of the Lark, The see He Loves You
Sportsman, A (Kol-pa) [467] 123
Star, The see To-Tole
Stranger Baby (Ya-cha Ka-wy) [548] 136

Tale-o with Squirrels [465] 122
Talking Fawn see Indian Child with Fawn
To-Tole, The Star [23] 34, 35, 96
Today [148] 65
Tom with a Jack Rabbit [116] 65
Topsy (Kol-pi-ta) [678] 90, 152
Trade Day [158] 65, 88
Trouble (Pi-shu-din) [337] 118
Tullo's Boy Dubert [622] 140
Turnip Baby, The [17] 32, 33
Two Indian Children (Kati-brin and Ka-tum) [601] 143

Ud-dool, The Only One [426] 77
Ukiah Treasures see Yokia Treasures
Ukiah Treasures 34
Untitled 34, 36, 41, 65, 137

War Eagle, The (Shai) [478] 126
Warfield Mitchell [316] 68
Wayside Flowers [500] 70
We Got Him [466] 79
When the Birds Went to War [580] 144
While the Hops Ripen [147] 65
Whispering Leaves, The [155] 53, 102
Who Comes (Cho-ba Wa-dee) [28] 36, 94
Wi-ly, The [412] 74
Wild Pigeon, The (Chi-bot-ta) [475] 80
Wild Roses 70

Ya-cha Ka-wy see Stranger Baby
Ya-cha Ka-wy 88
Yesterday [149] 106
Yokia Treasures [20] 34, 95